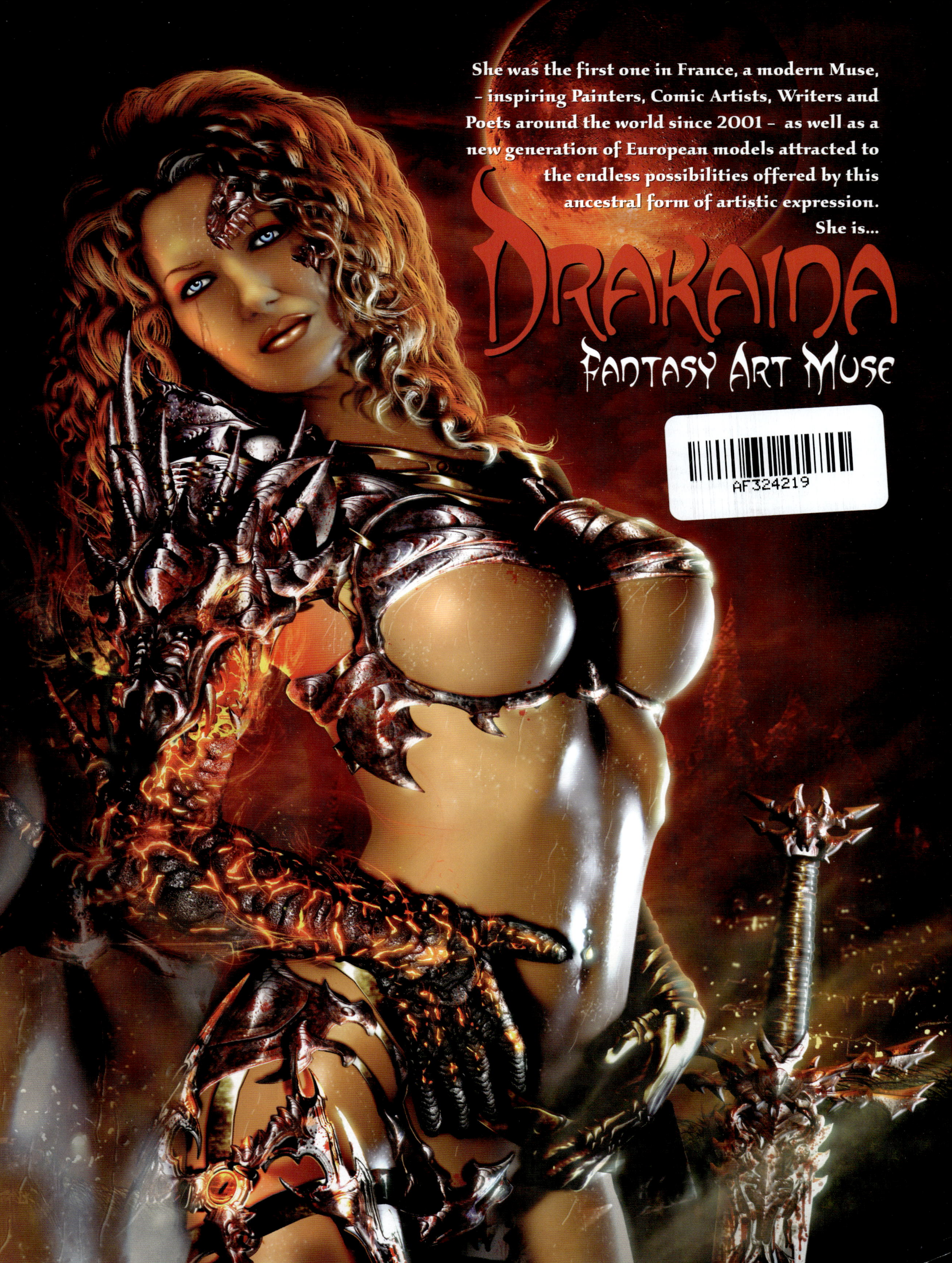

She was the first one in France, a modern Muse,
– inspiring Painters, Comic Artists, Writers and
Poets around the world since 2001 – as well as a
new generation of European models attracted to
the endless possibilities offered by this
ancestral form of artistic expression.
She is…

DRAKAINA
FANTASY ART MUSE

AF324219

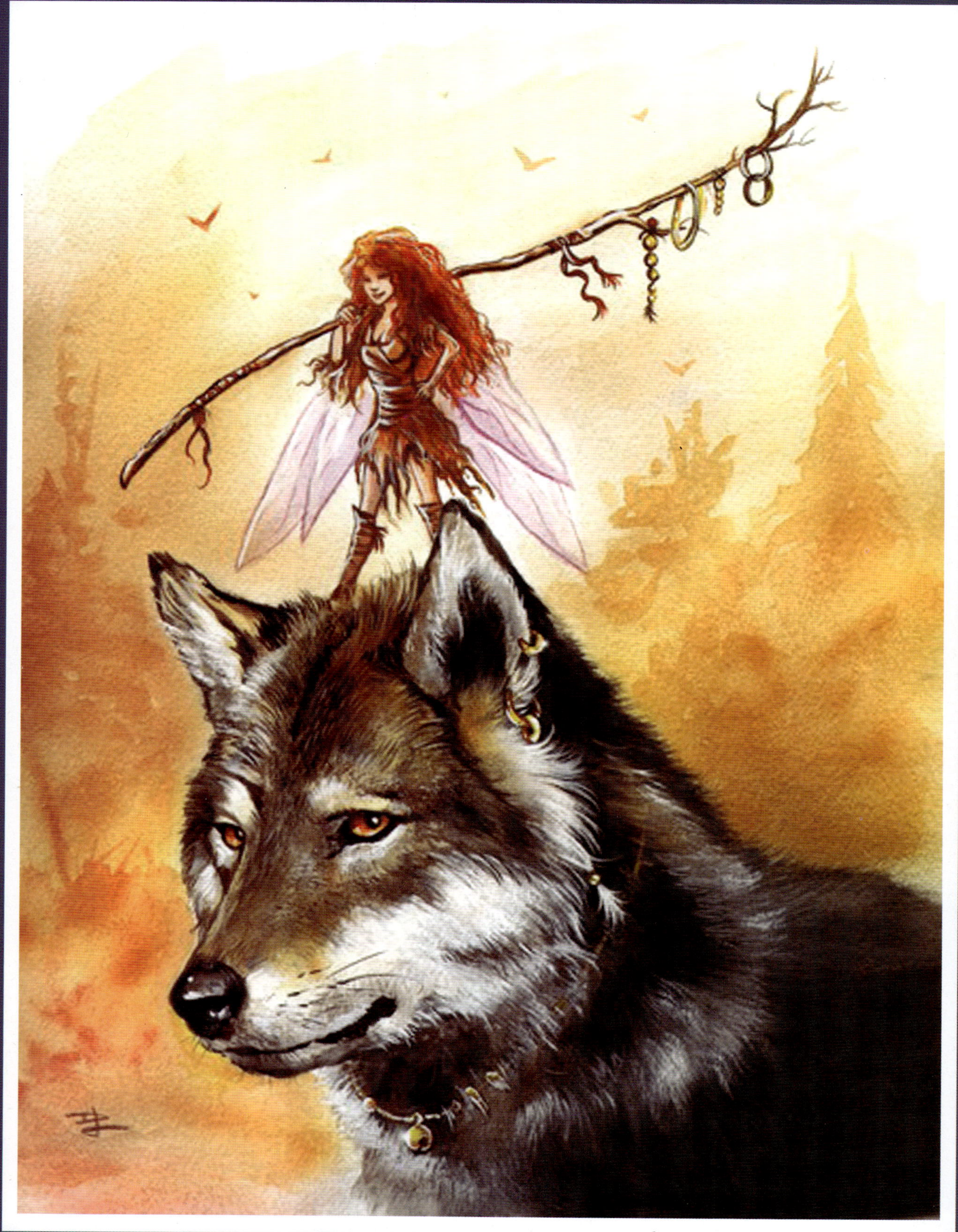

Art by Denis Lapierre

http://www.denis-lapierre.com/

"Dogs always held a special place in my heart and and this is why today, being in the "public eye" I do my best to fight for their rights and well-being by asking people to be aware of how badly these loving creatures are being abused around the world, sometimes no further than in the yard next door"

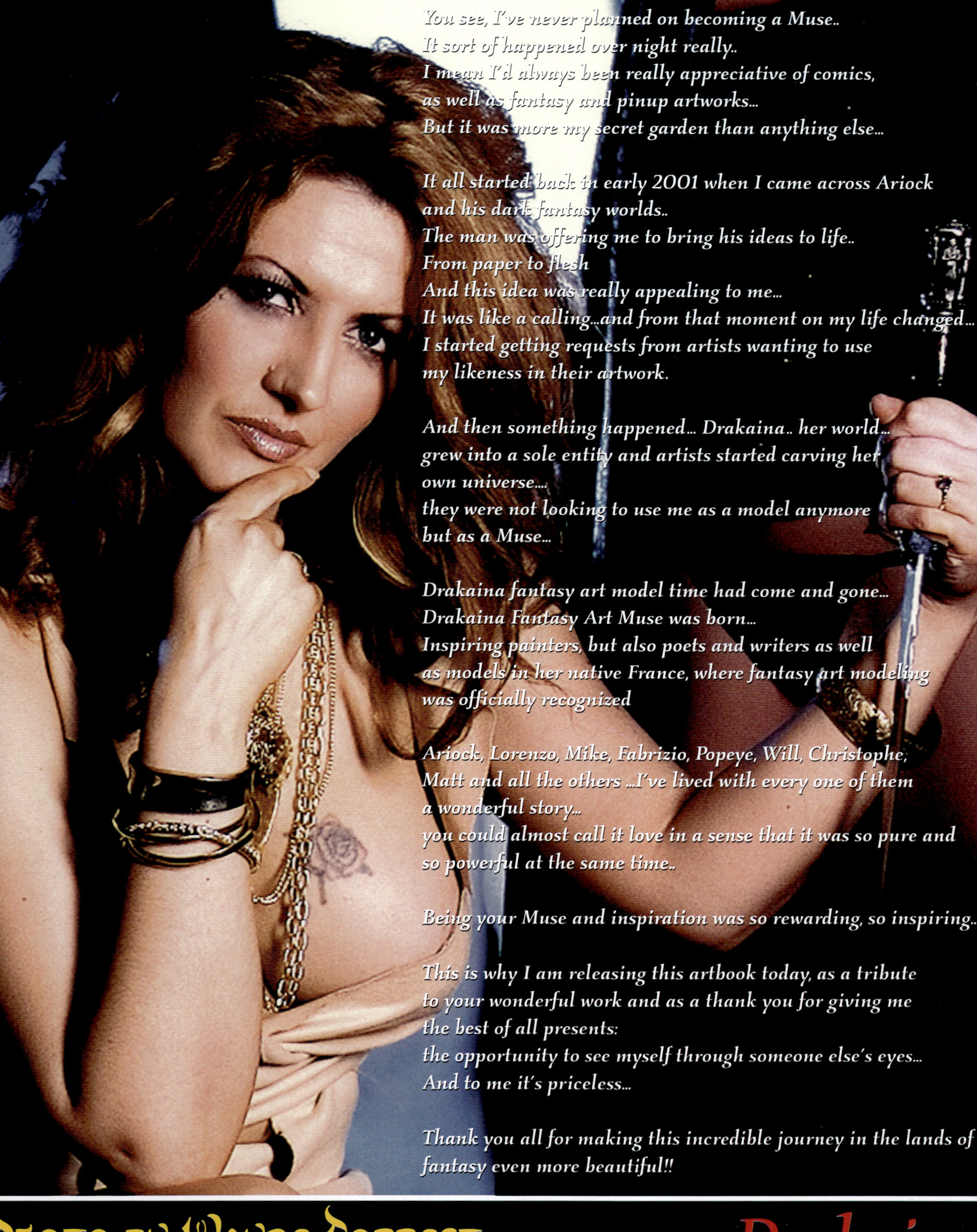

You see, I've never planned on becoming a Muse..
It sort of happened over night really..
I mean I'd always been really appreciative of comics,
as well as fantasy and pinup artworks...
But it was more my secret garden than anything else...

It all started back in early 2001 when I came across Ariock
and his dark fantasy worlds..
The man was offering me to bring his ideas to life..
From paper to flesh
And this idea was really appealing to me...
It was like a calling...and from that moment on my life changed...
I started getting requests from artists wanting to use
my likeness in their artwork.

And then something happened... Drakaina.. her world...
grew into a sole entity and artists started carving her
own universe....
they were not looking to use me as a model anymore
but as a Muse...

Drakaina fantasy art model time had come and gone...
Drakaina Fantasy Art Muse was born...
Inspiring painters, but also poets and writers as well
as models in her native France, where fantasy art modeling
was officially recognized

Ariock, Lorenzo, Mike, Fabrizio, Popeye, Will, Christophe,
Matt and all the others ...I've lived with every one of them
a wonderful story...
you could almost call it love in a sense that it was so pure and
so powerful at the same time..

Being your Muse and inspiration was so rewarding, so inspiring...

This is why I am releasing this artbook today, as a tribute
to your wonderful work and as a thank you for giving me
the best of all presents:
the opportunity to see myself through someone else's eyes...
And to me it's priceless...

Thank you all for making this incredible journey in the lands of
fantasy even more beautiful!!

Photo by Wayne Forrest
http://gmesh.deviantart.com/

Drakaina

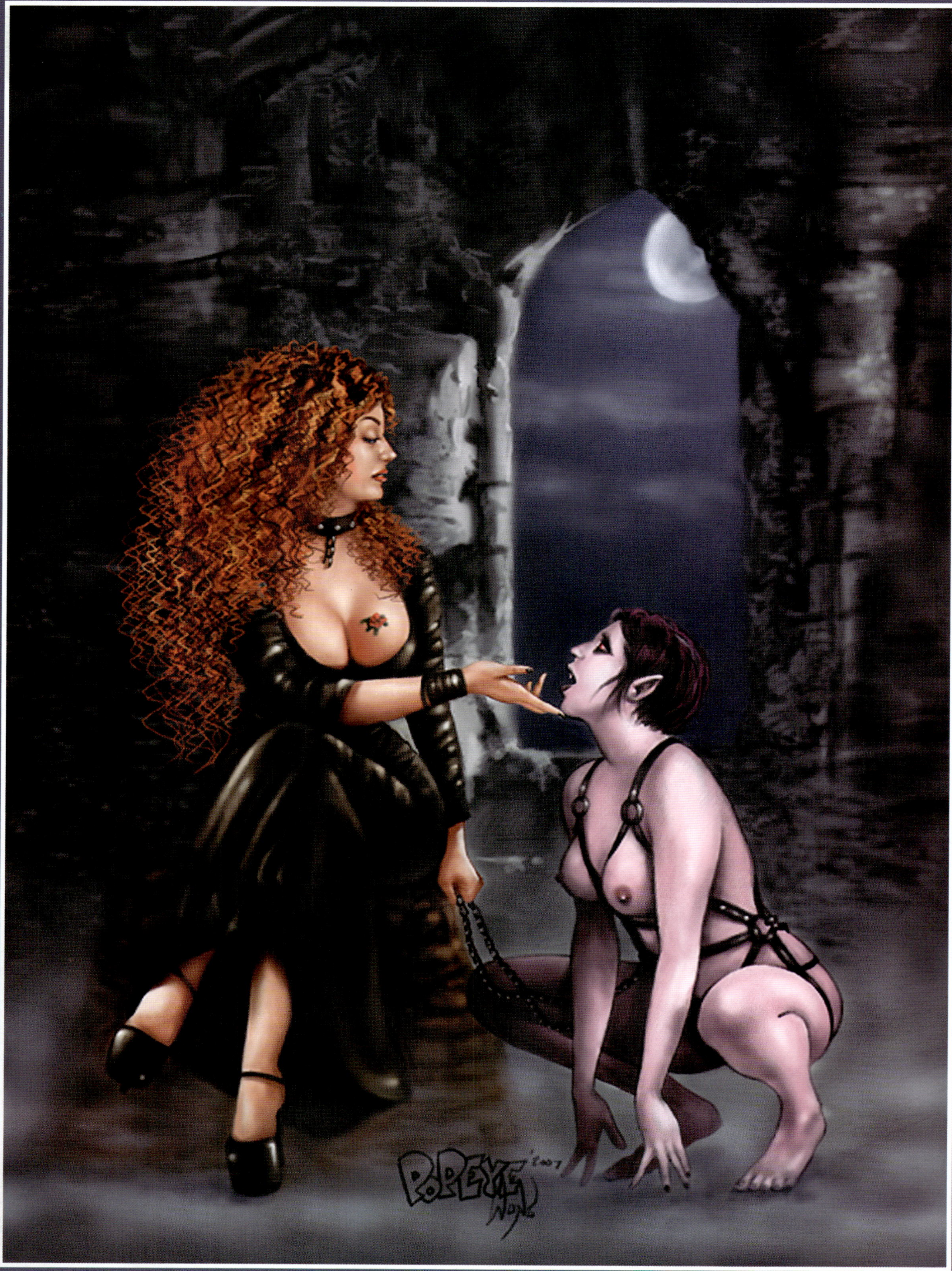

DRAKAINA BY POPEYE WONG

<http://www.popeyewong.com/>

How does Drakaina inspire me as a muse? Since the first time I did an artwork with her, the characteristic that immediately grabbed my attention was her amazonian-warrior-meets-statuesque-princess physique. Just looking at that beautiful mass of red curly hair, and those majestic breasts complemented with a red rose tattoo on one of them, would be enough to make more than one artist drool. Of course, that is not her only asset, and in my opinion, it is not even the most important one. Drakaina also projects a powerful grace that is not easy to find in any given model. What truly inspires me, is the attitude she has towards her work, especially modeling for Fantasy artwork. You can tell how much of a passion she has for the Fantasy genre, because she genuinely shares and projects that passion in front of the camera. I worked with Drakaina for the first time in 2004 and I still get the same inspiration every time I work with her

"As you see, the art of my dear friend Popeye ranges from cute pin-ups to fantasy art paintings. We have been working together since 2004 and I must say than his style changed quite a bit along the years. His drawings are now reaching the maturity of the great fantasy artists he has always admired. Working with him is always a pleasure."

image. I like to do erotic and sometimes dark artwork, and Drakaina hits the right spot in both areas. She has the talent, the elements, the body, and she's not afraid to show them all at once. That attitude is what I am looking for in any model that I work with, therefore, every time I have the chance to work with Drakaina I get great pleasure out of the experience.

I give reverence and thanks to a true Muse: Drakaina

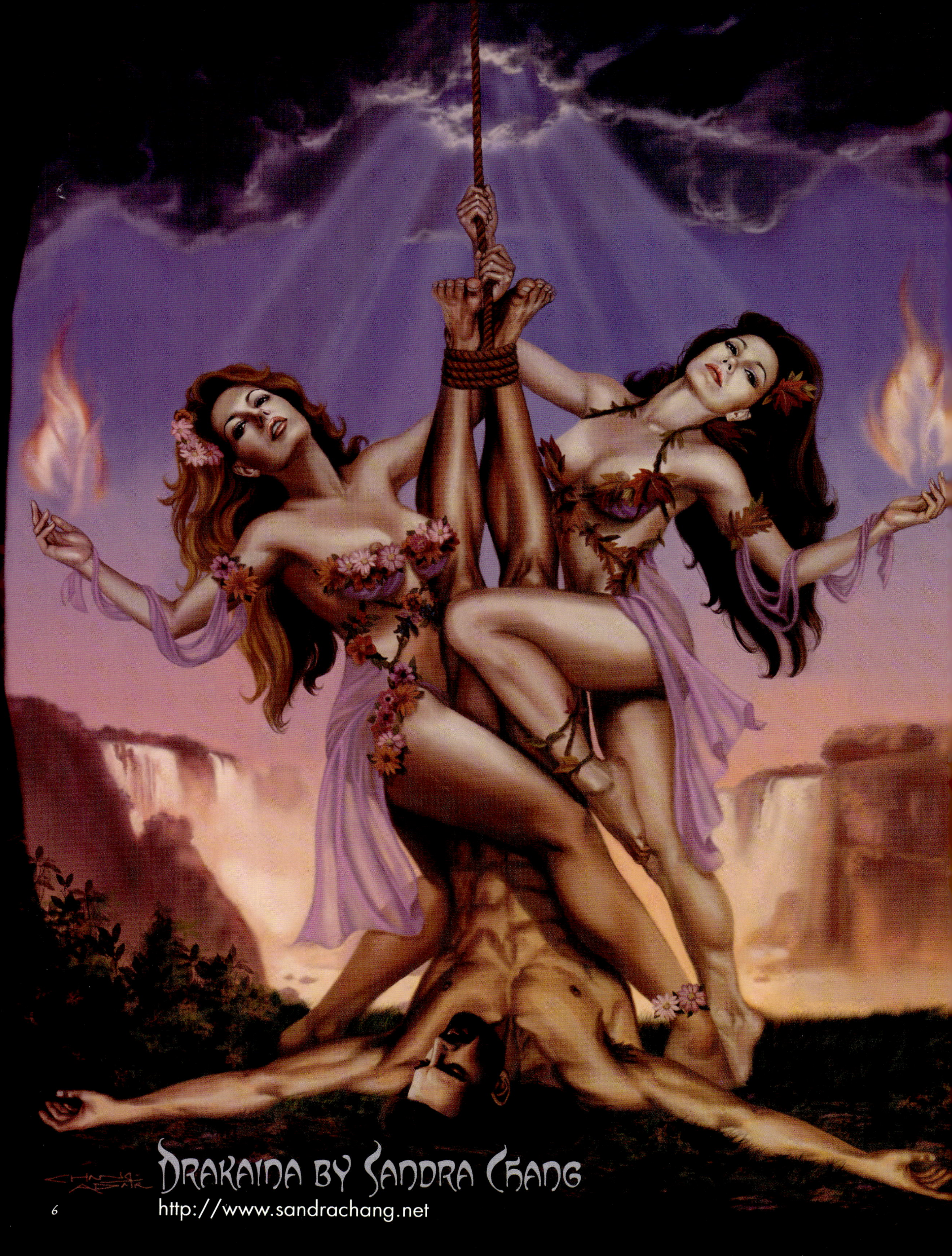

DRAKAINA BY SANDRA CHANG
http://www.sandrachang.net

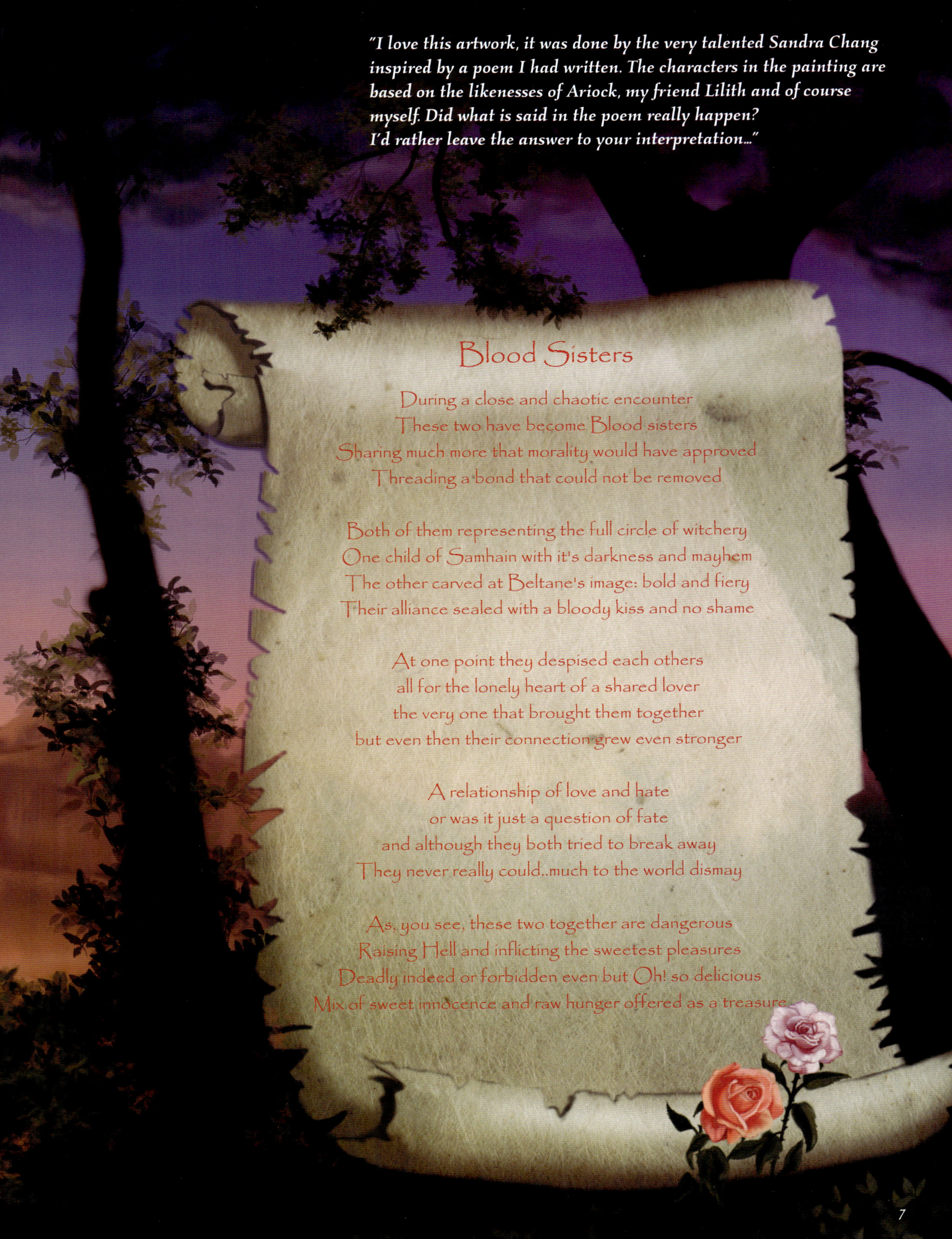

"I love this artwork, it was done by the very talented Sandra Chang
inspired by a poem I had written. The characters in the painting are
based on the likenesses of Ariock, my friend Lilith and of course
myself. Did what is said in the poem really happen?
I'd rather leave the answer to your interpretation..."

Blood Sisters

During a close and chaotic encounter
These two have become Blood sisters
Sharing much more that morality would have approved
Threading a bond that could not be removed

Both of them representing the full circle of witchery
One child of Samhain with it's darkness and mayhem
The other carved at Beltane's image: bold and fiery
Their alliance sealed with a bloody kiss and no shame

At one point they despised each others
all for the lonely heart of a shared lover
the very one that brought them together
but even then their connection grew even stronger

A relationship of love and hate
or was it just a question of fate
and although they both tried to break away
They never really could..much to the world dismay

As, you see, these two together are dangerous
Raising Hell and inflicting the sweetest pleasures
Deadly indeed or forbidden even but Oh! so delicious
Mix of sweet innocence and raw hunger offered as a treasure

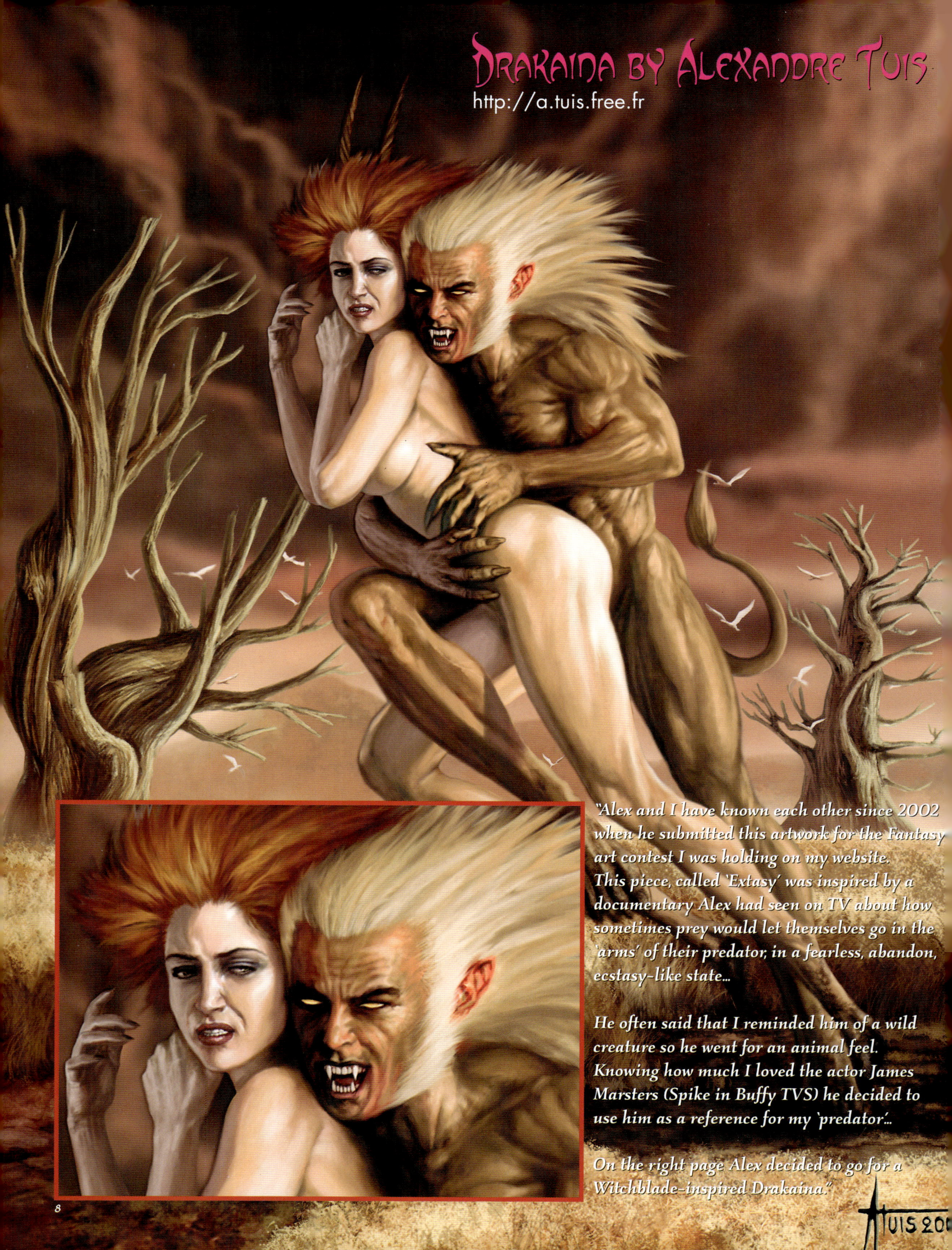

"Alex and I have known each other since 2002 when he submitted this artwork for the Fantasy art contest I was holding on my website. This piece, called 'Extasy' was inspired by a documentary Alex had seen on TV about how sometimes prey would let themselves go in the 'arms' of their predator, in a fearless, abandon, ecstasy-like state…

He often said that I reminded him of a wild creature so he went for an animal feel. Knowing how much I loved the actor James Marsters (Spike in Buffy TVS) he decided to use him as a reference for my 'predator'…

On the right page Alex decided to go for a Witchblade-inspired Drakaina."

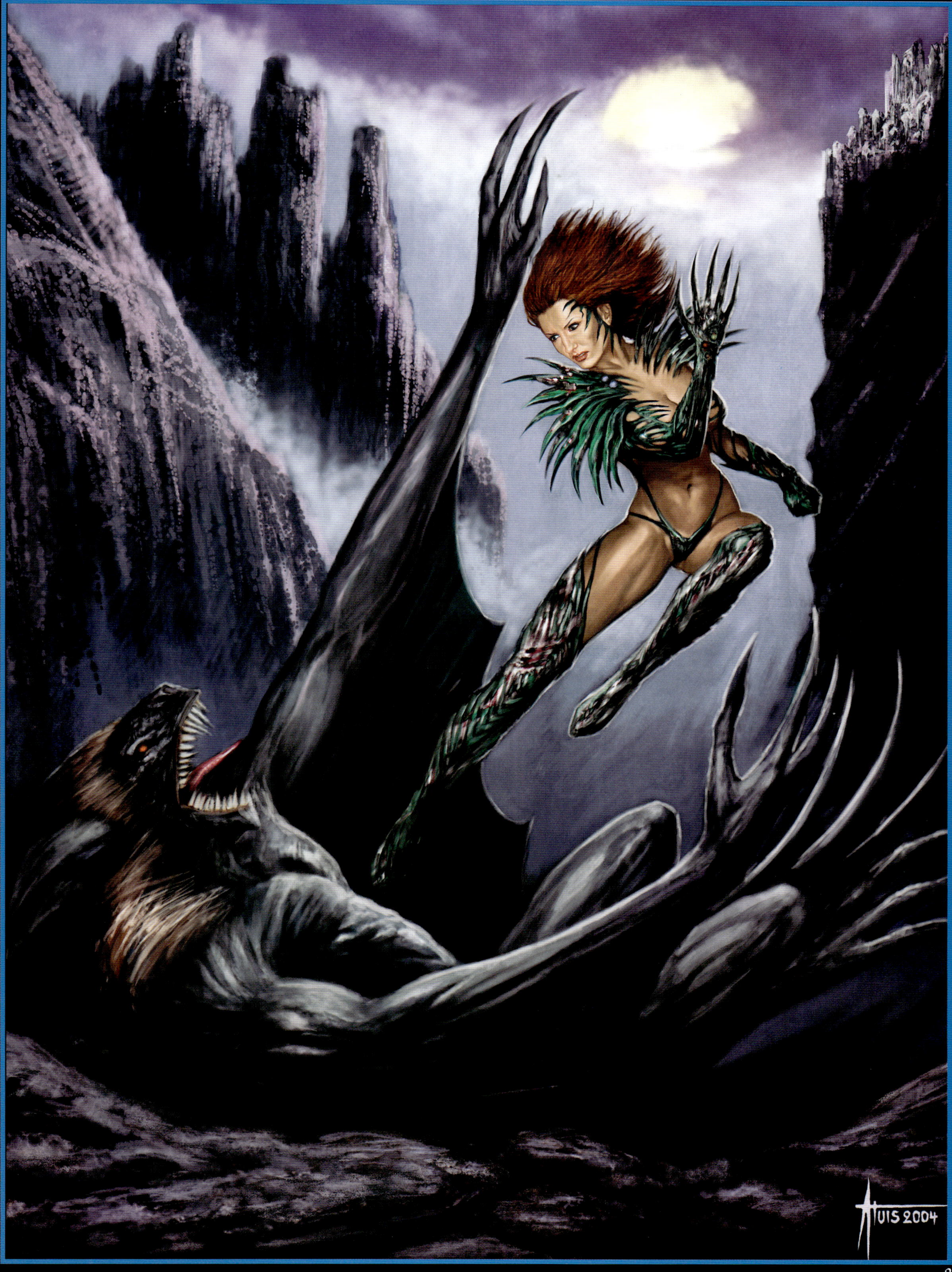
Luis 2004

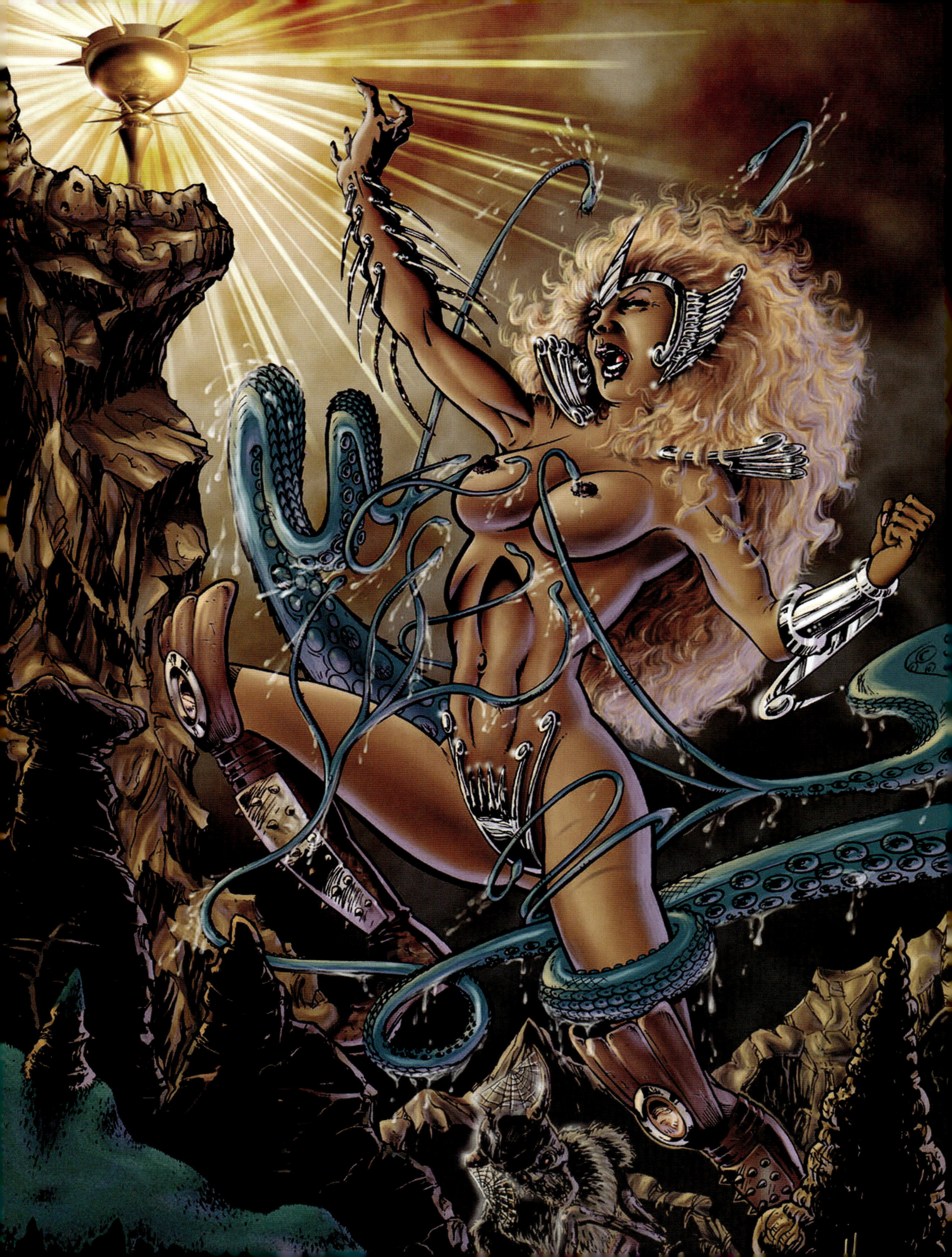

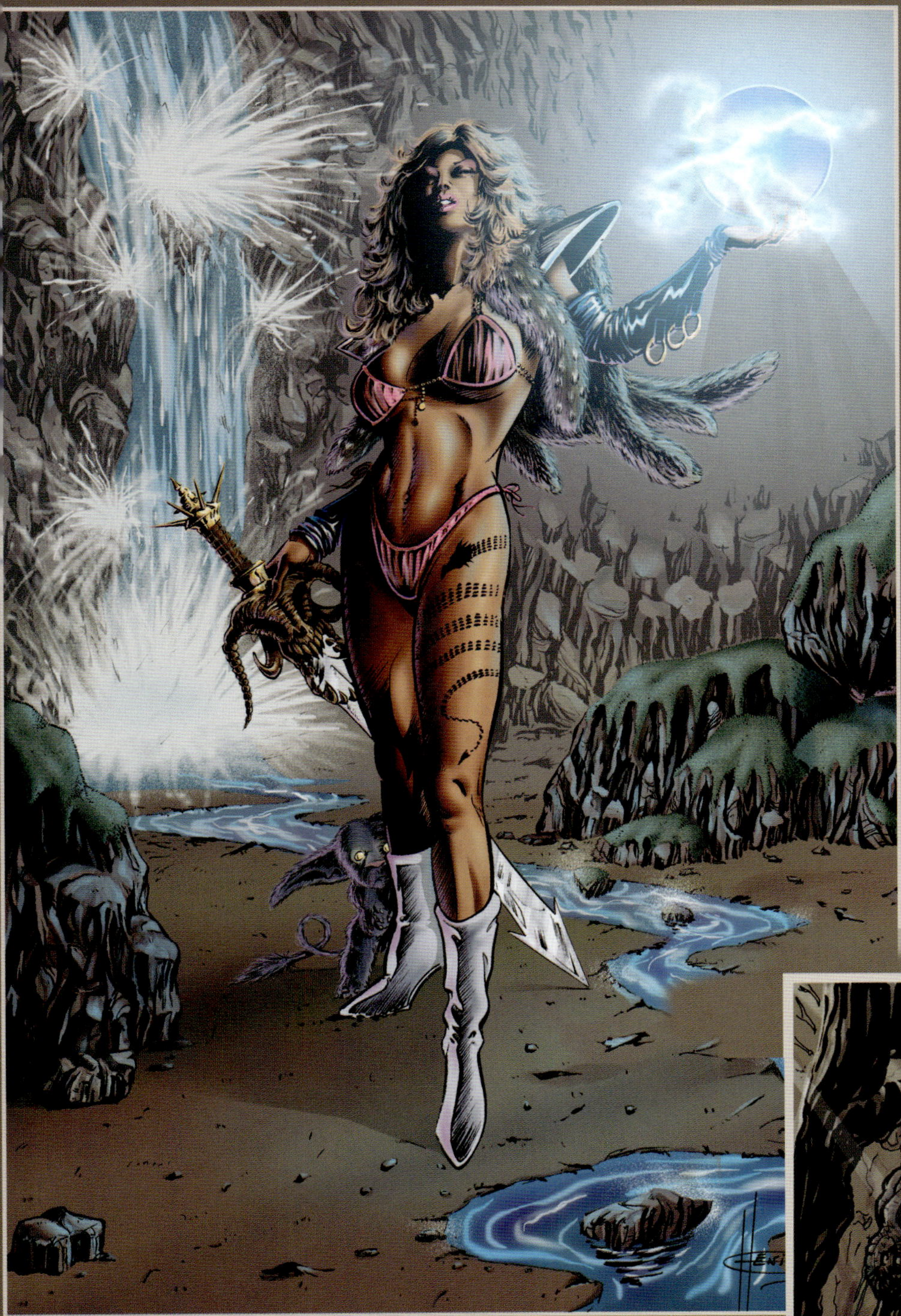

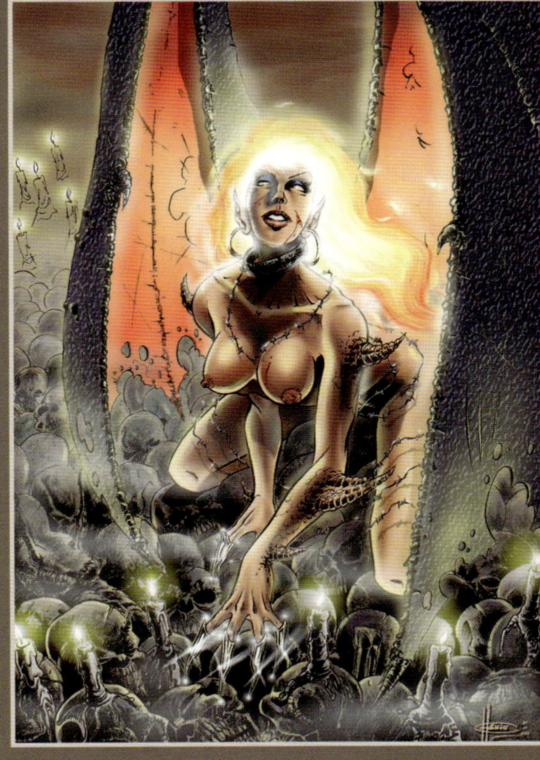

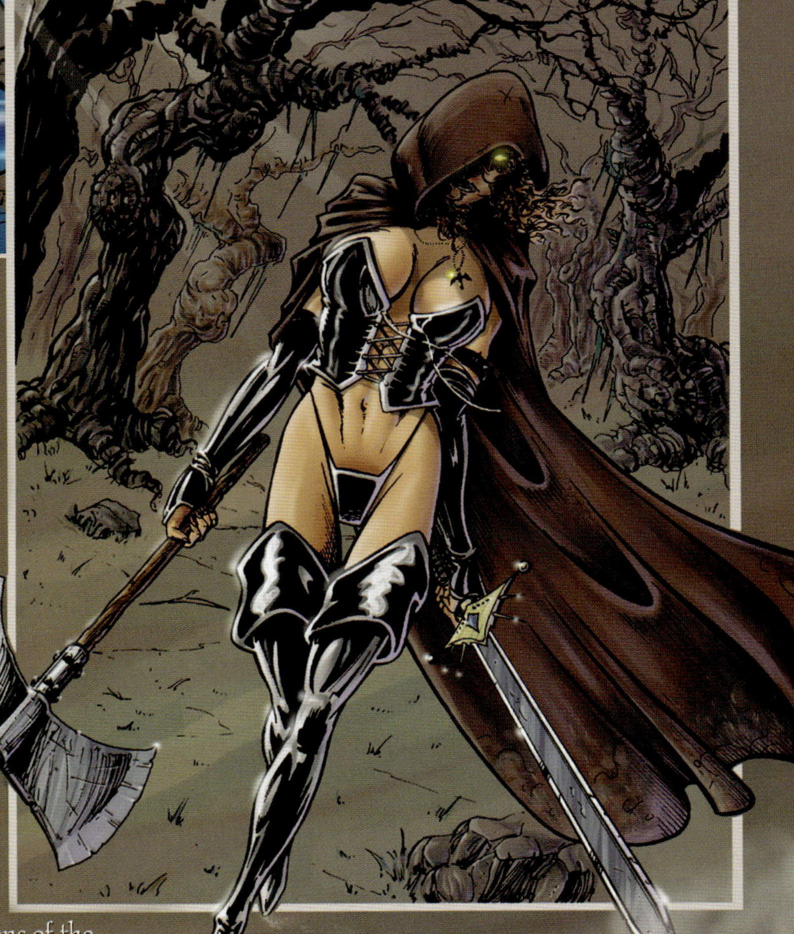

Drakaina by Christophe Henin

http://perso.wanadoo.fr/christophe.henin.art

I first saw Drakaina on a TV show, in which she was talking about her "Fantasy Art Model" job, and then, I discovered her universe, a mix of eroticism, fantasy, sensibility, mysticism and war-strength. I e-mailed her to have more information about her activity and to congratulate her. After seeing my website, she said she really liked my work and my style, and offered me to do illustrations of her character "Drakaina". It was the beginning of our collaboration. I did my first pin up for her (Drakaina Power Light) from a picture on her site, keeping most of the posture, but changing the arms positions. Drak' said to me she really loved this drawing. So, I went ahead with other art for her in that fashion. Unlike other artists who do pin-ups from her pictures and manage to redo the posture by adding their universe, I prefer to totally re-create the layout, the posture, where I add my own vision of the character, by taking inspiration from feelings, colors, stature of several pics. So, I really do illustrations of the "Concept" of Drakaina, more than real illustrations of the character itself.

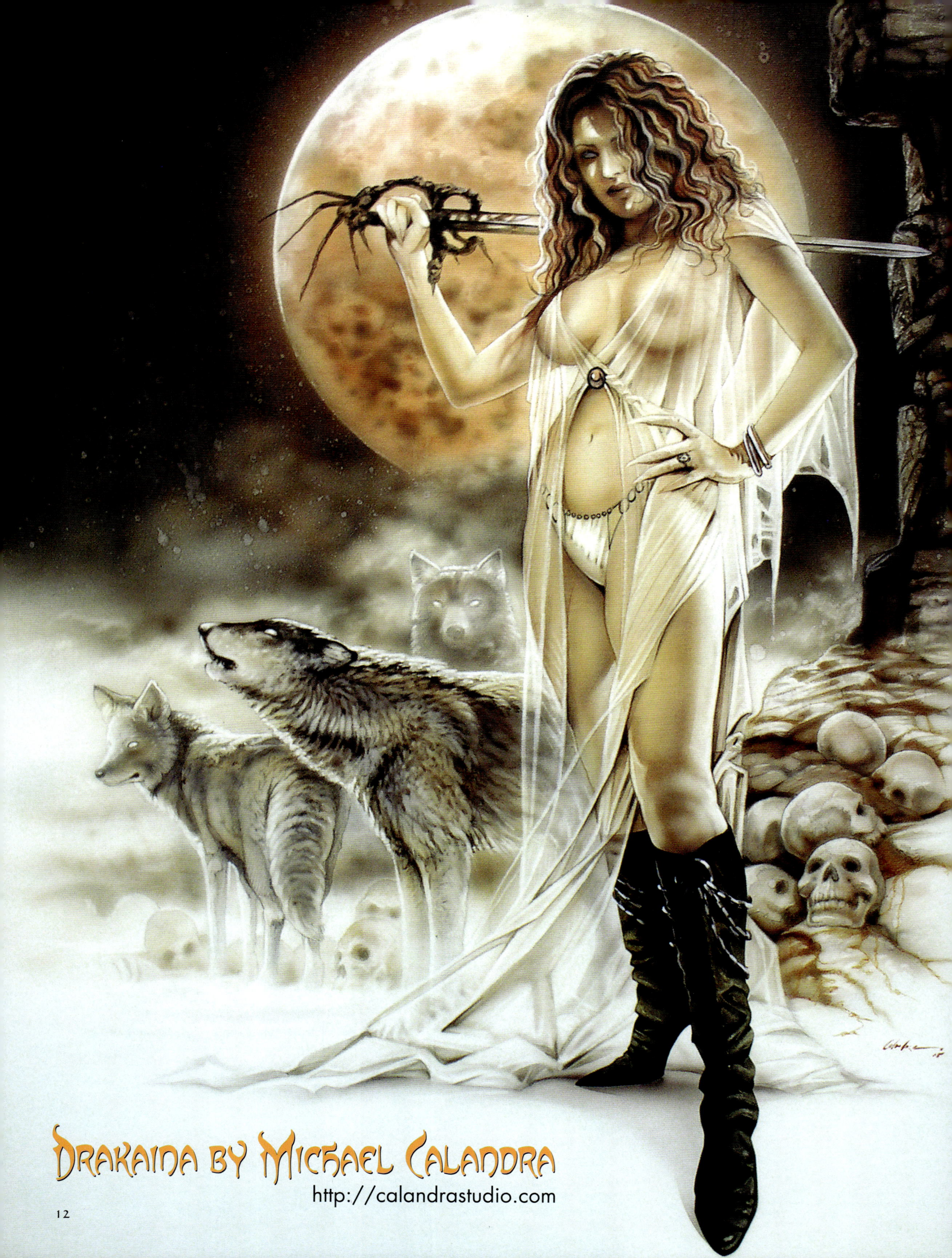

Drakaina by Michael Calandra
http://calandrastudio.com

I always try to capture the essence of my subjects in
their environment, so I always look for models that
have the ability to project themselves on film.

Drakaina not only has the classic beauty of a fantasy
model, but also has ability to leave a bit of her
personal magic in her images.

By doing this, she inspires many artists to envision
her in fantasy worlds, often leading the way as a
heroic, strong female presence.

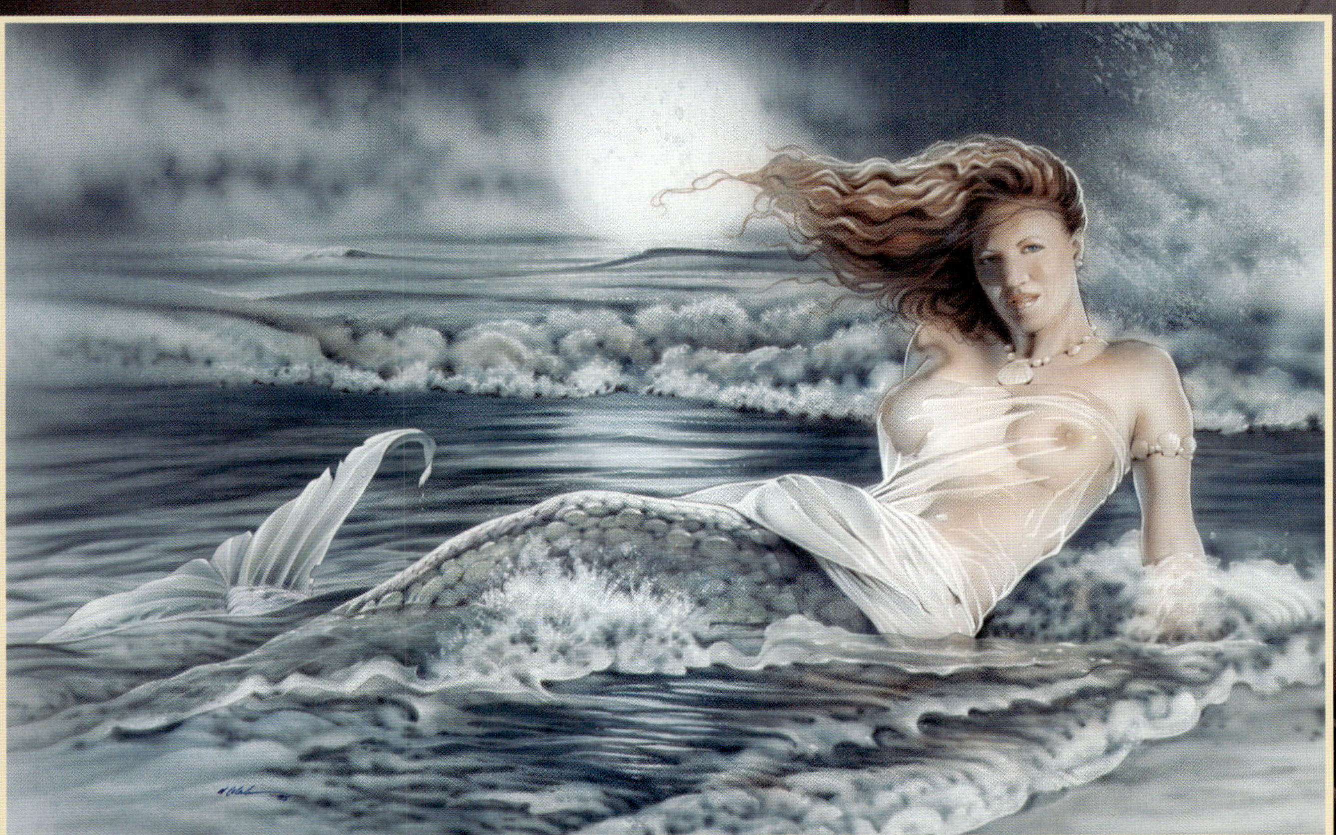

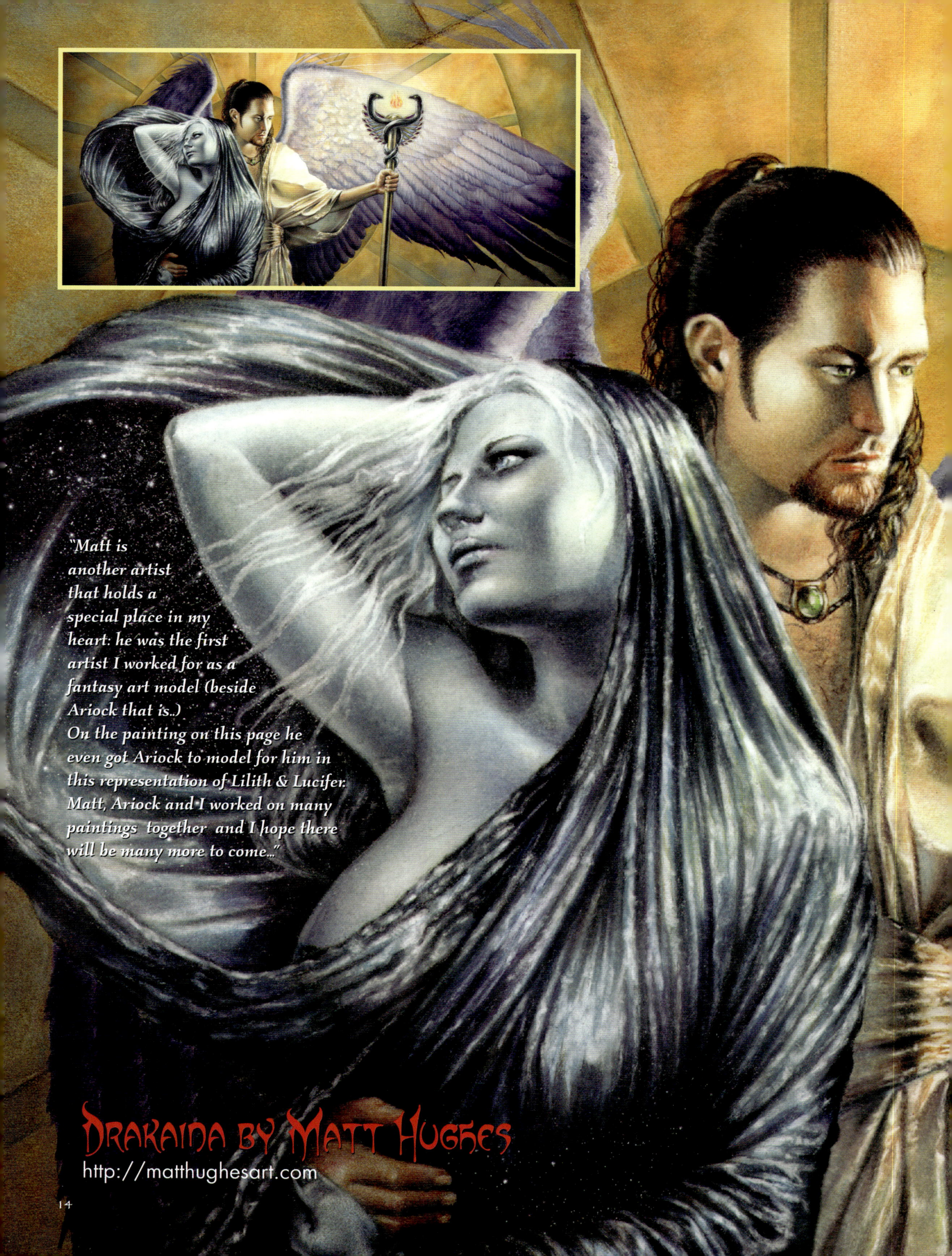

DRAKAIDA BY MATT HUGHES
http://matthughesart.com

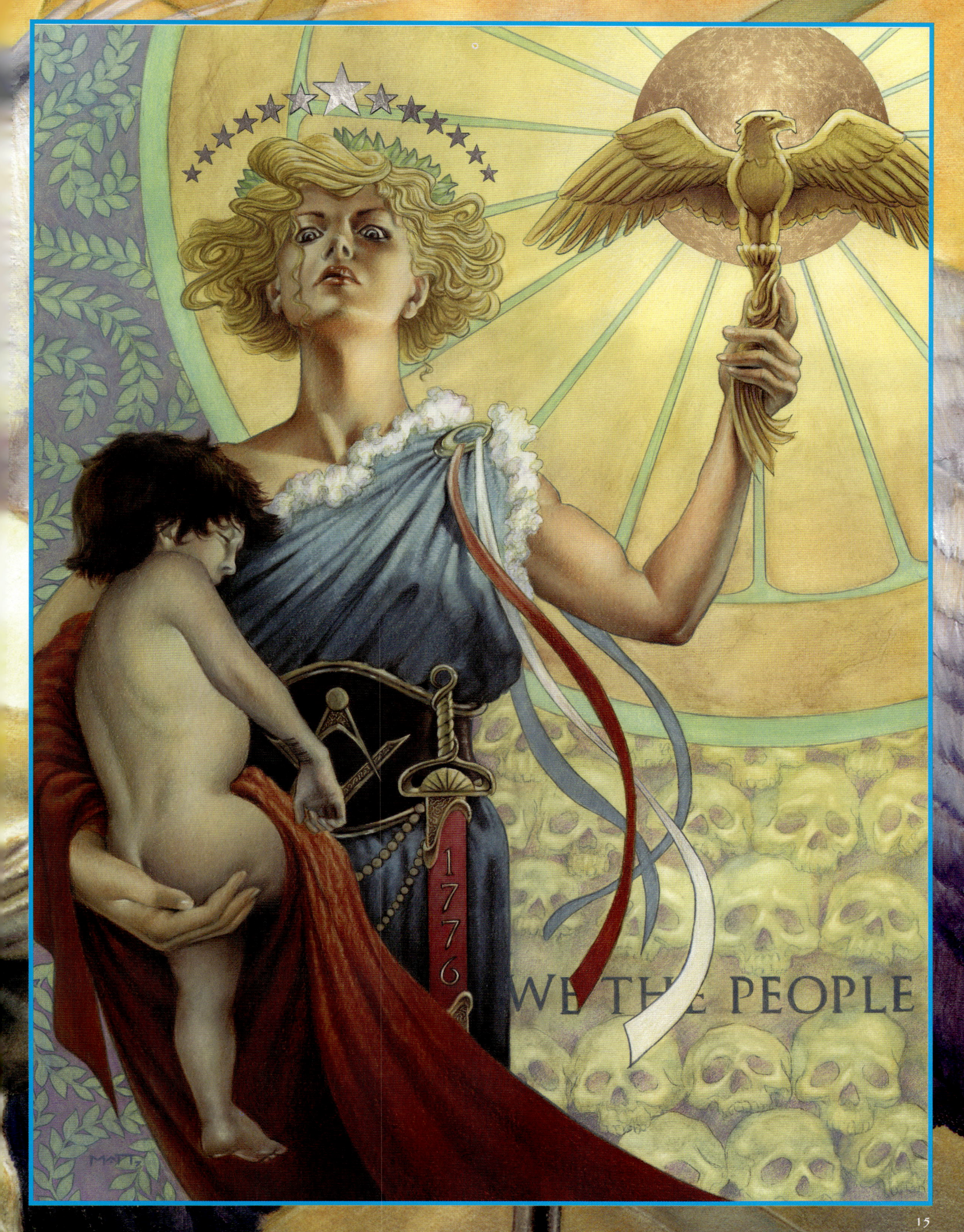

1776
WE THE PEOPLE

"More artworks from Matt, with the reference pictures he used. I usually don't show the reference pictures used by the artists but in Matt's case it is different as, as I said on the previous page, he was the first artist using me as a fantasy art model besides Ariock.

Ariock was a great help in starting my fantasy art modeling career as, on top of being a very good photographer he also created all the props and costumes himself, which made my job much easier.

Below is a picture of Ariock and I for the Lilith painting, and I think it was Ariock's very first time as a fantasy art model. Good times..."

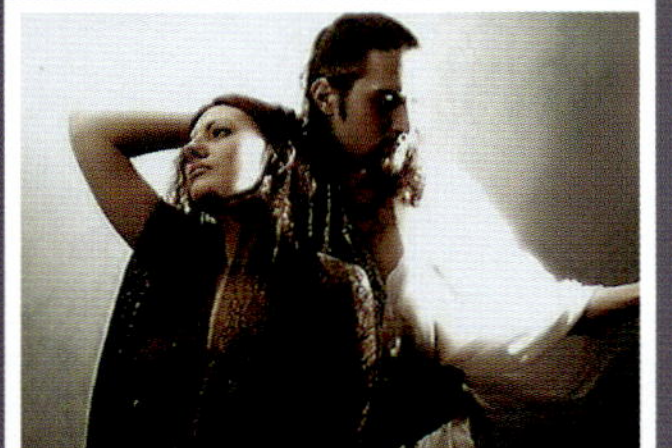

"Boudicca was Queen of the Inceni around 40 AD There are numerous legends regarding her courage and leadership. In 40 AD she led a revolt against the governing Roman empire which had occupied her region for decades.
This illustration is part 2 of a 3-part series that will depict both her courage and bravery against impossible odds.

This illustration premiered at the 2004 after Oscar's party for Lord of the Rings –
The Return of the King"

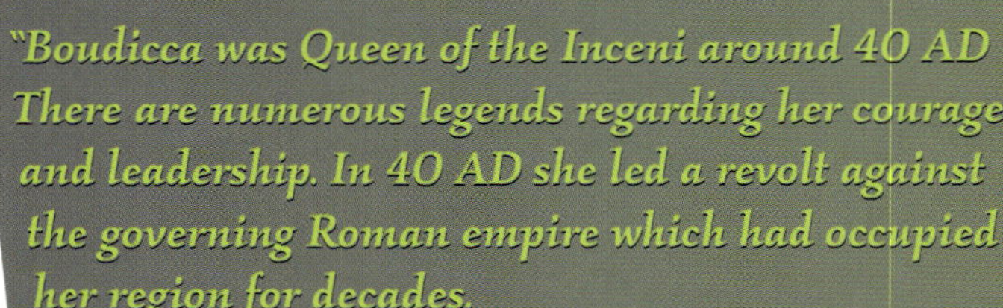

Drakaina by Queen Boudicca

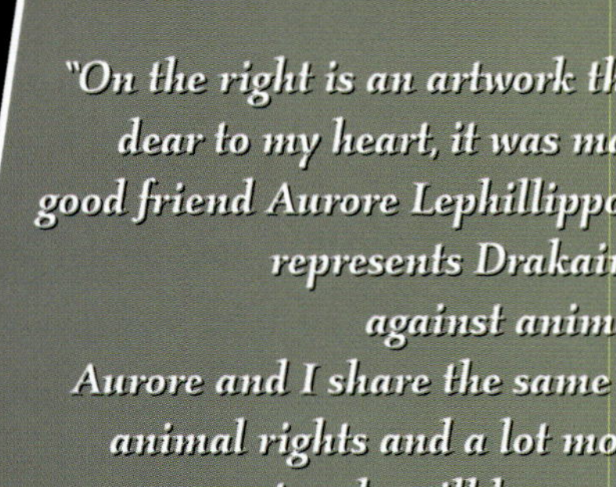

"On the right is an artwork that is very dear to my heart, it was made by my good friend Aurore Lephillipponnat and represents Drakaina's stand against animal cruelty.
Aurore and I share the same values on animal rights and a lot more related artworks will be coming soon."

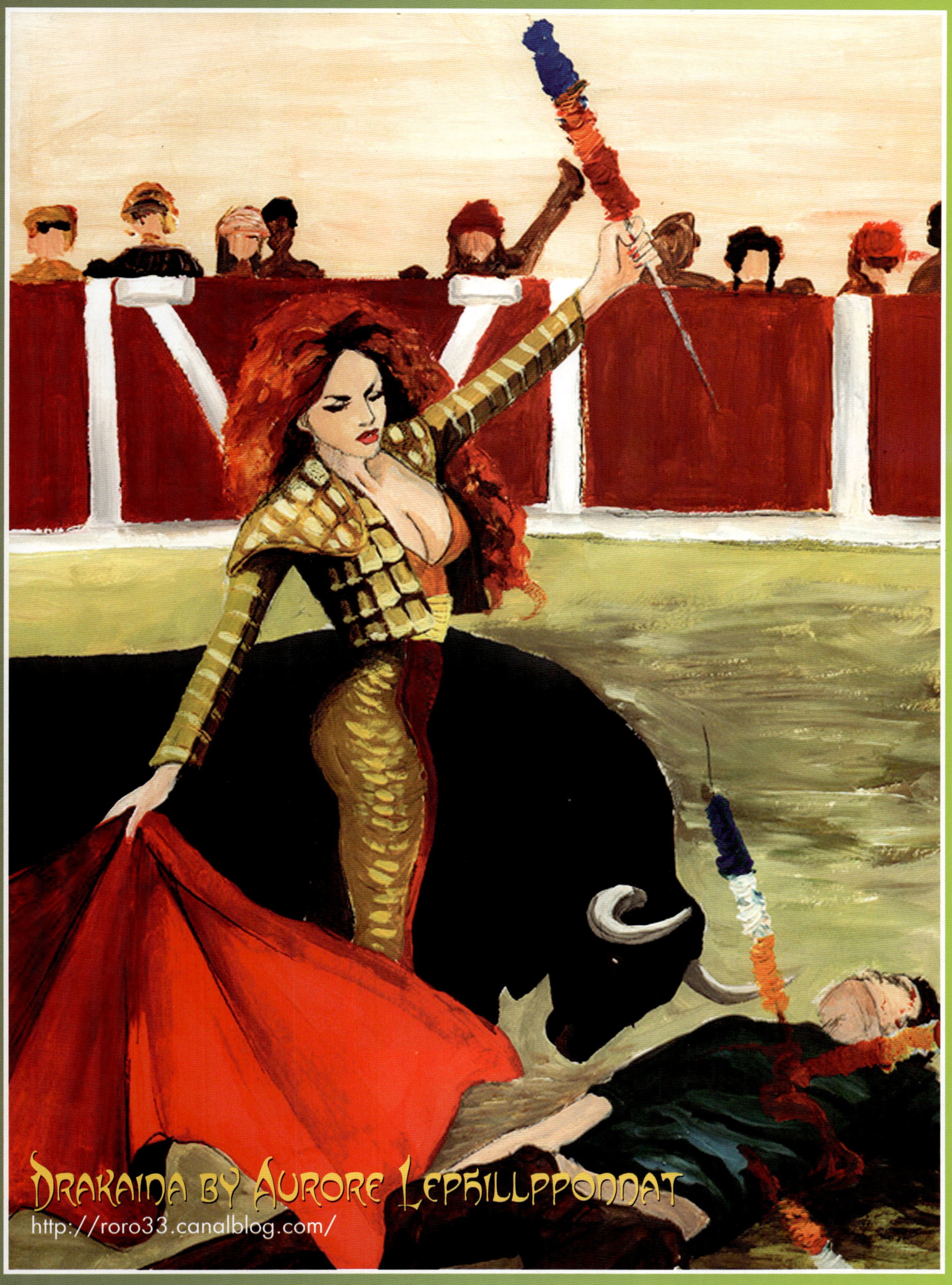

Drakaina by Aurore Lephillppondat
http://roro33.canalblog.com/

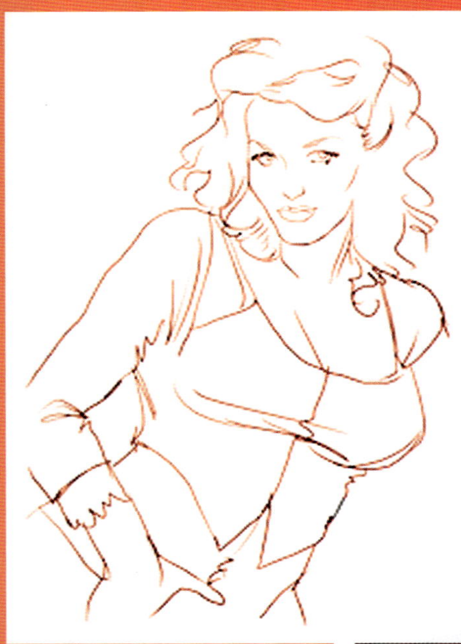
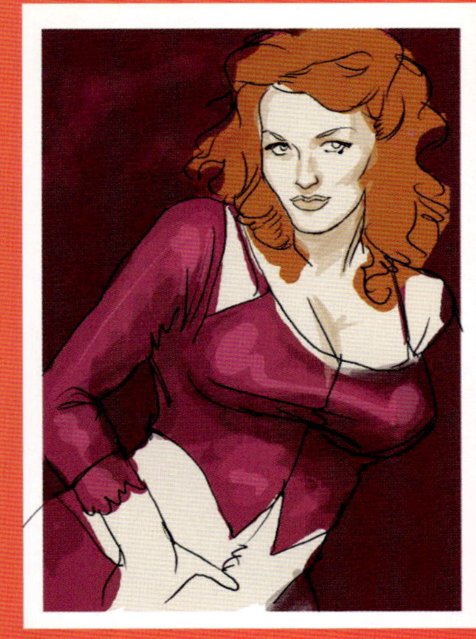
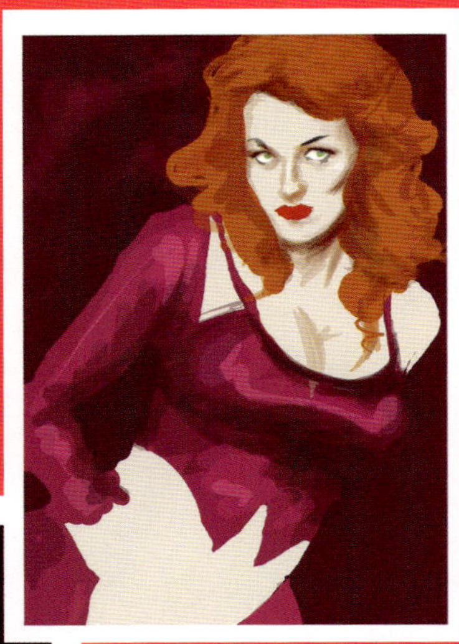
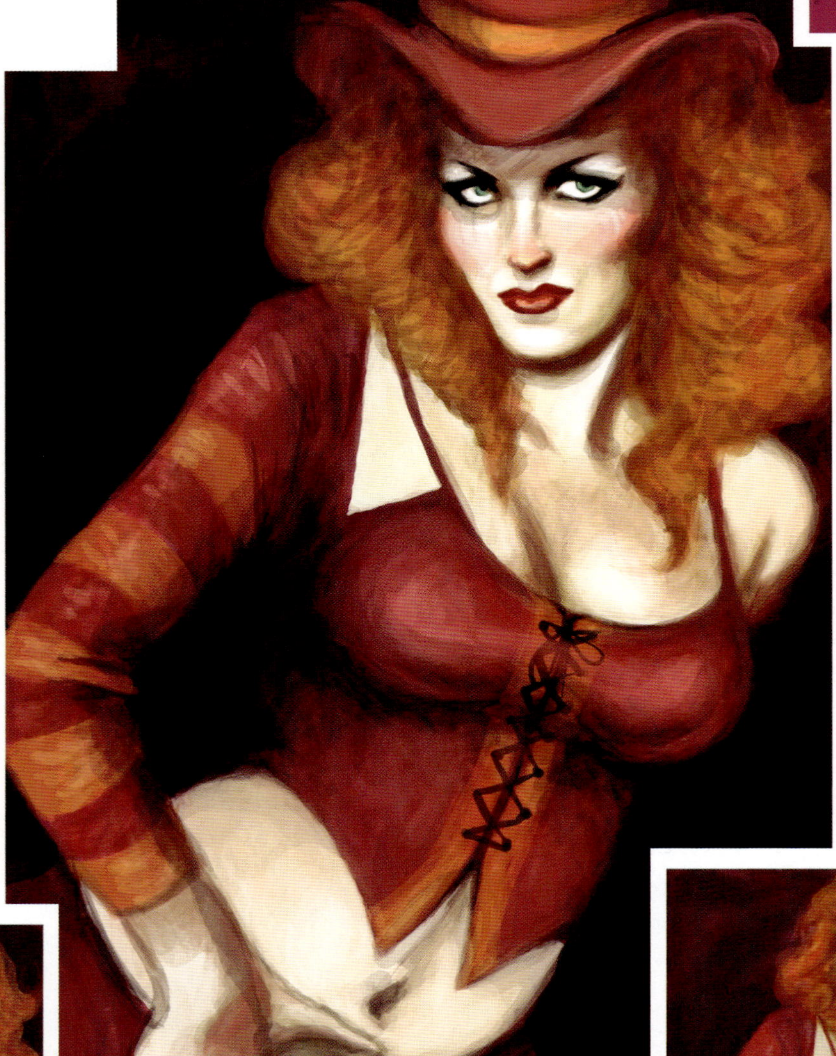
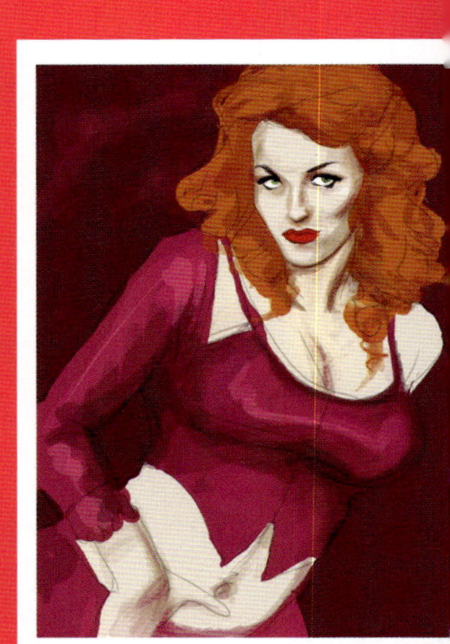
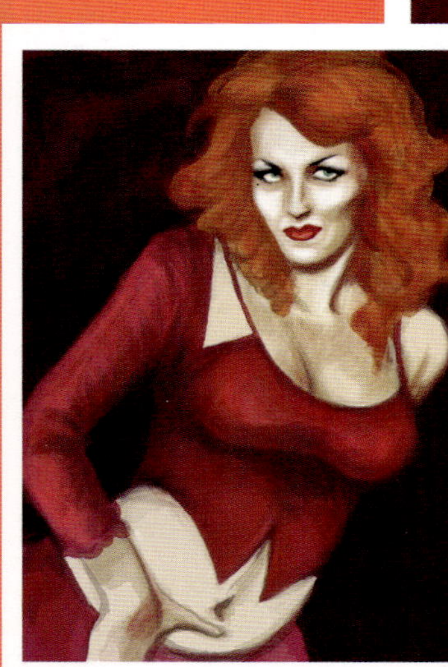
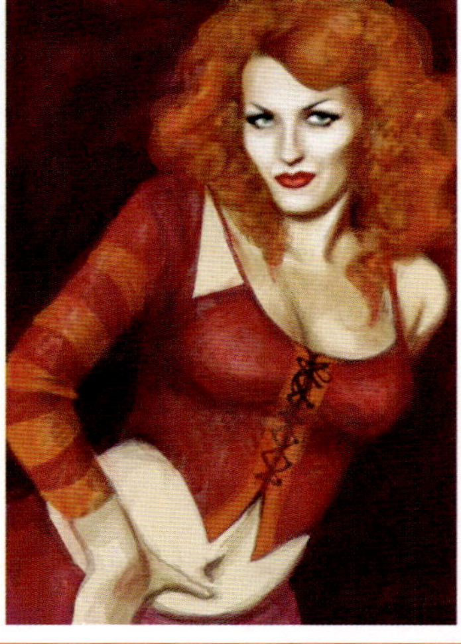

Drakaina by Aurore Lephilipponnat
http://roro33.canalblog.com/

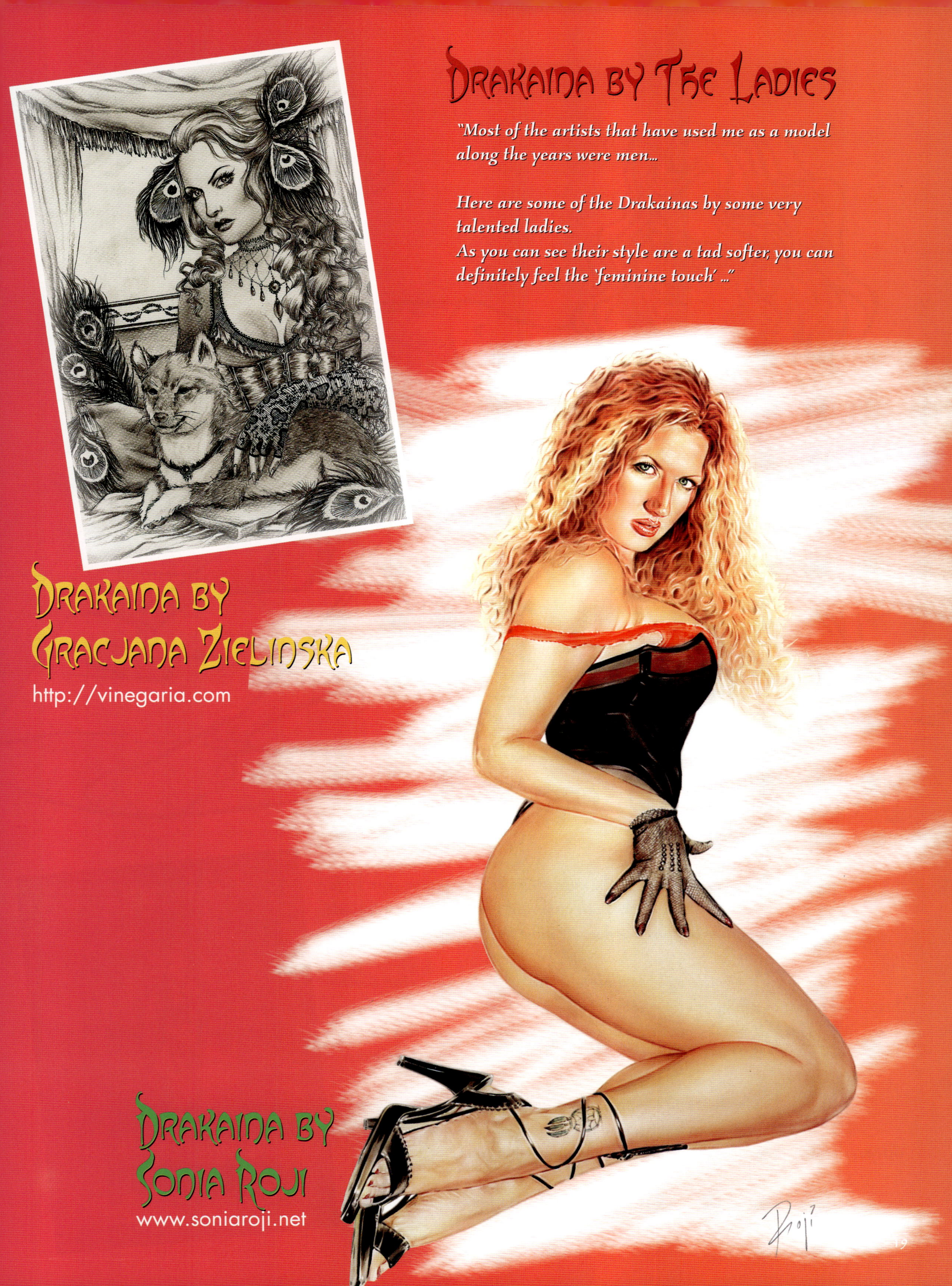

DRAKAINA BY THE LADIES

"Most of the artists that have used me as a model along the years were men...

Here are some of the Drakainas by some very talented ladies.
As you can see their style are a tad softer, you can definitely feel the 'feminine touch' ..."

DRAKAINA BY
GRACJANA ZIELINSKA
http://vinegaria.com

DRAKAINA BY
SONIA ROJI
www.soniaroji.net

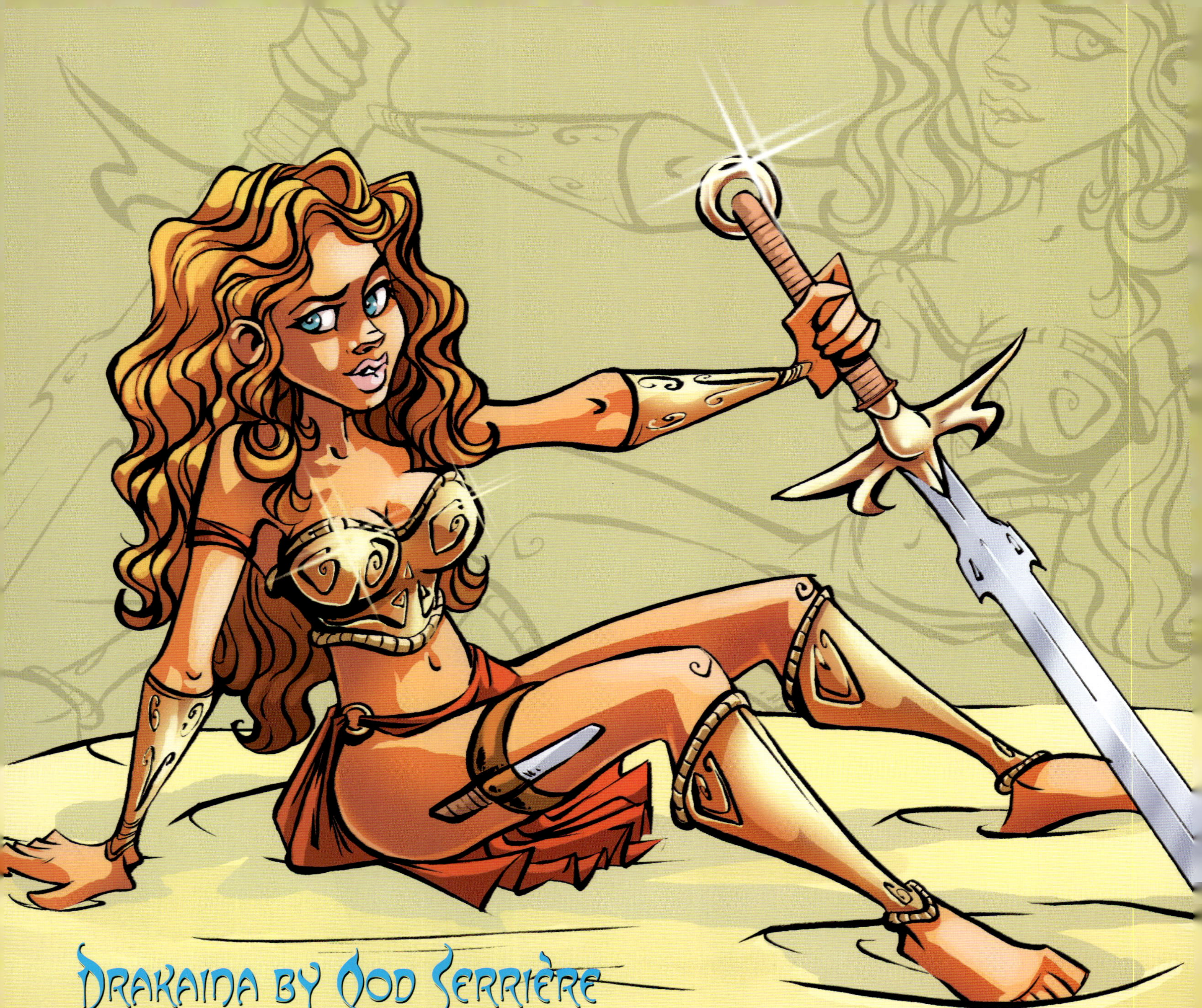

Drakaina by Ood Serrière

http://ood-ood.blogspot.com

"Ood's Drakaina is one of the cutest Drakainas I have seen so far, she looks both cute and ready to stir up trouble. Unlike other images she doesn't have that sultry warrior look."

"To the right is a bloody Drakaina by Sandrine Berthe (http://sabbook.canalblog.com/), another cutie. Don't you just love the furry seat?? It makes me think of cousin Itt from the Addams Family and makes me smile every single time."

"On the opposite page are 3 black & white nudes by Bry (http://la-griffe-de-bry.com) on the top left, Dino Idrizbegovic (http://illustrasite.com), top right and Eacone (www.eacone.com), bottom."

"Once again 3 very different views on Drakaina"

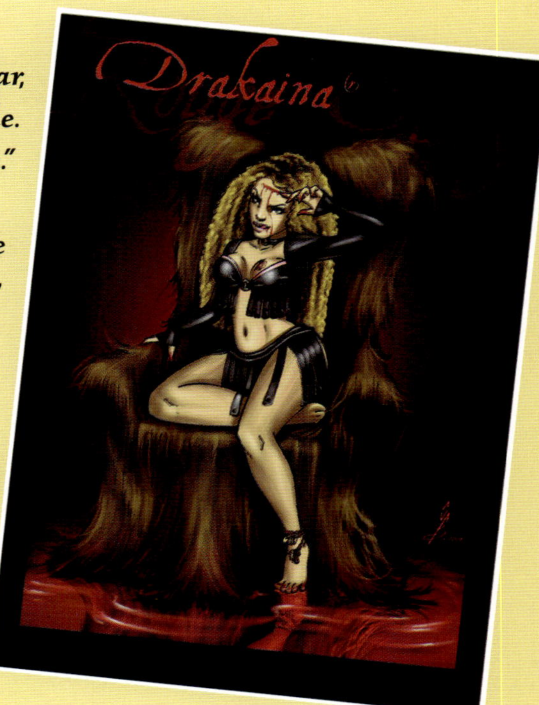

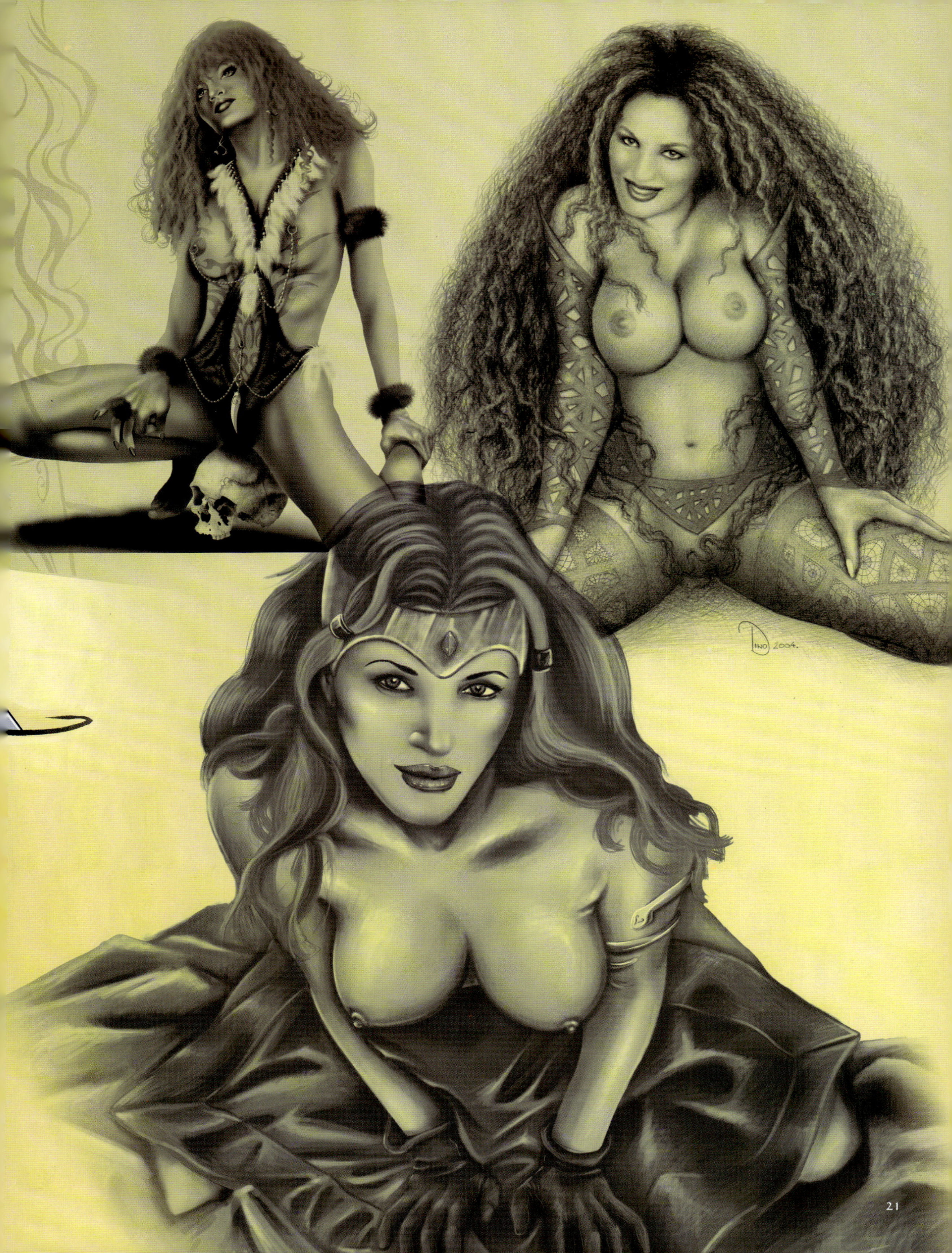

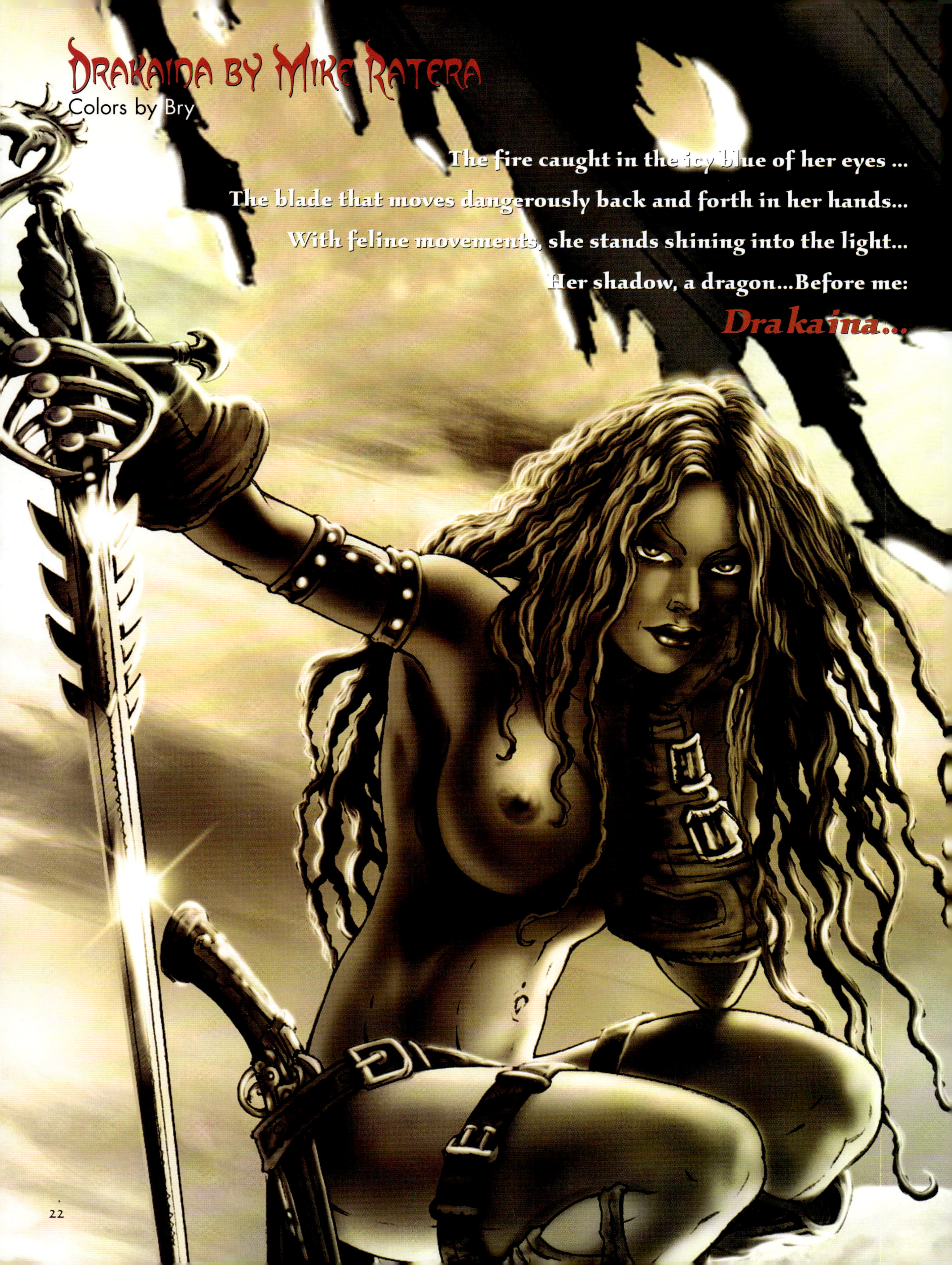

Drakaina by Mike Ratera
Colors by Bry

The fire caught in the icy blue of her eyes ...
The blade that moves dangerously back and forth in her hands...
With feline movements, she stands shining into the light...
Her shadow, a dragon...Before me:
Drakaina...

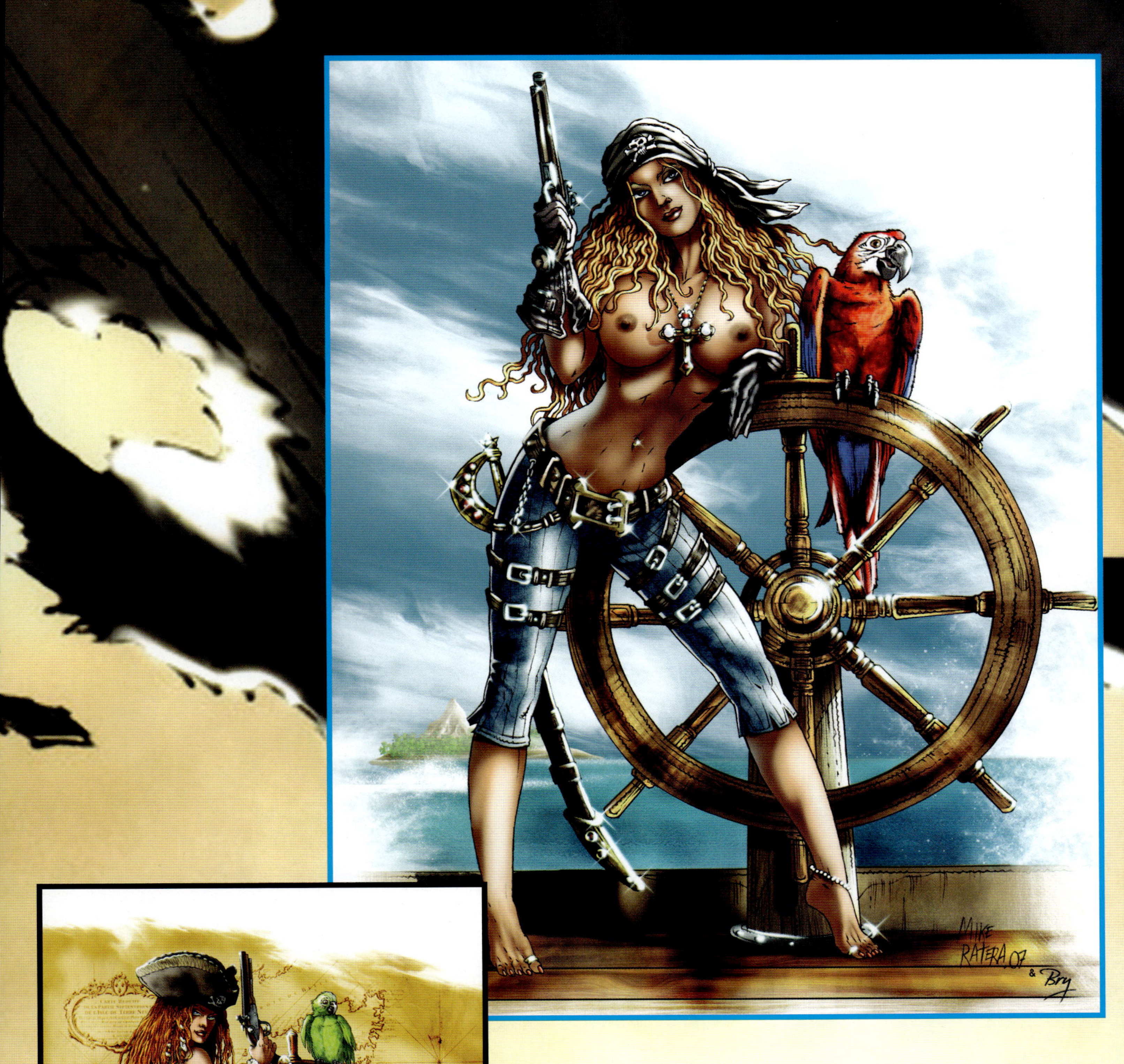

Drakaina Pirates

On left page is a preliminary version for one of the wonderful pirates by Mike Ratera.

Above and left are 2 of Mike's Pirates colored by Bry. Mike & Bry worked together for the artworks featured on both theses pages and the following two.

I study her movements...
begin to draw outlines on the sheet of paper
The Magic begins.
Once again.

It is beautiful to find someone of your kind,
someone so daring and passionate, not afraid to
embrace life to it's fullest, no matter the consequences...

And yet it is even more beautiful when it's a
woman with a great inner strength...
A woman capable of making your most
intimate dreams come true.

All that can be felt in Drakaina, as soon as you meet her.
A free spirit like the wind of the Great North ...
The secret desire to have wanted to live in another era ...
a very distant era... where magic was merged with
instinct and survival.

Here is the dream... Here is the vision...

Here is Drakaina.

Mike Ratera 2007

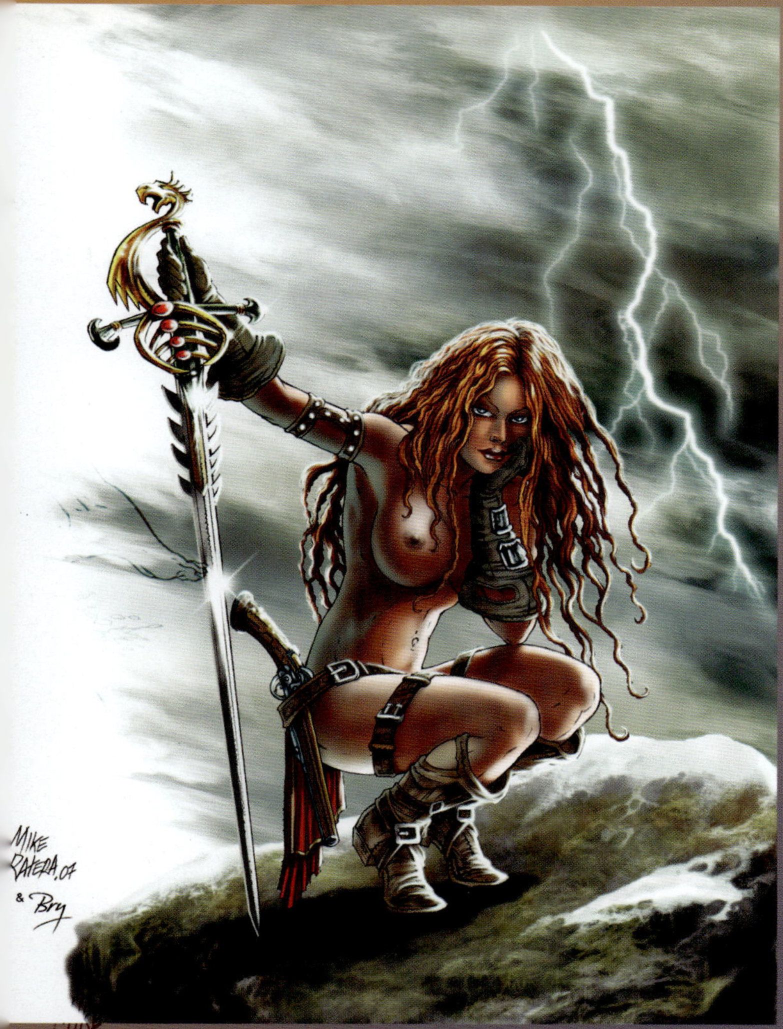
MIKE RATERA.07
& Bry

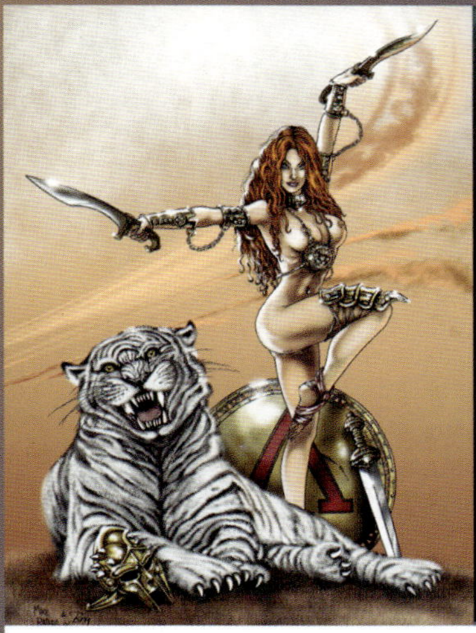

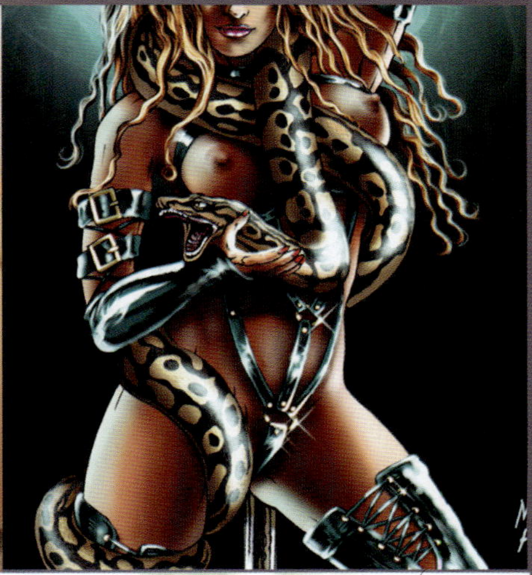

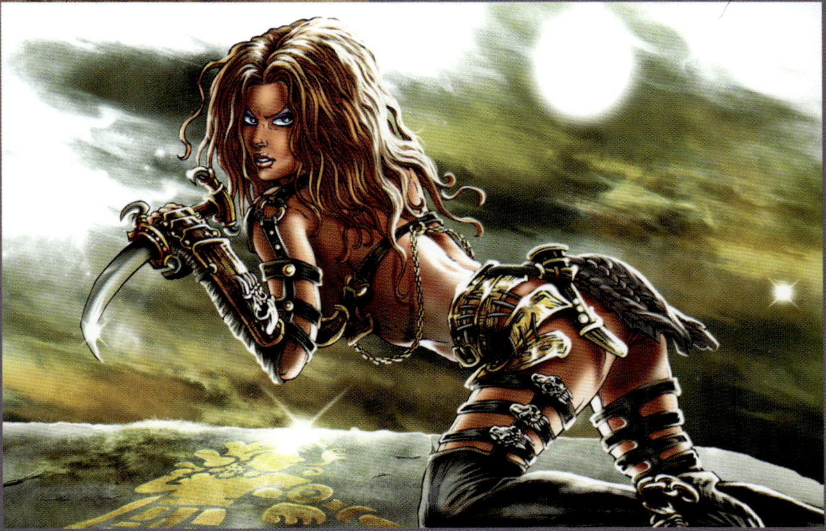

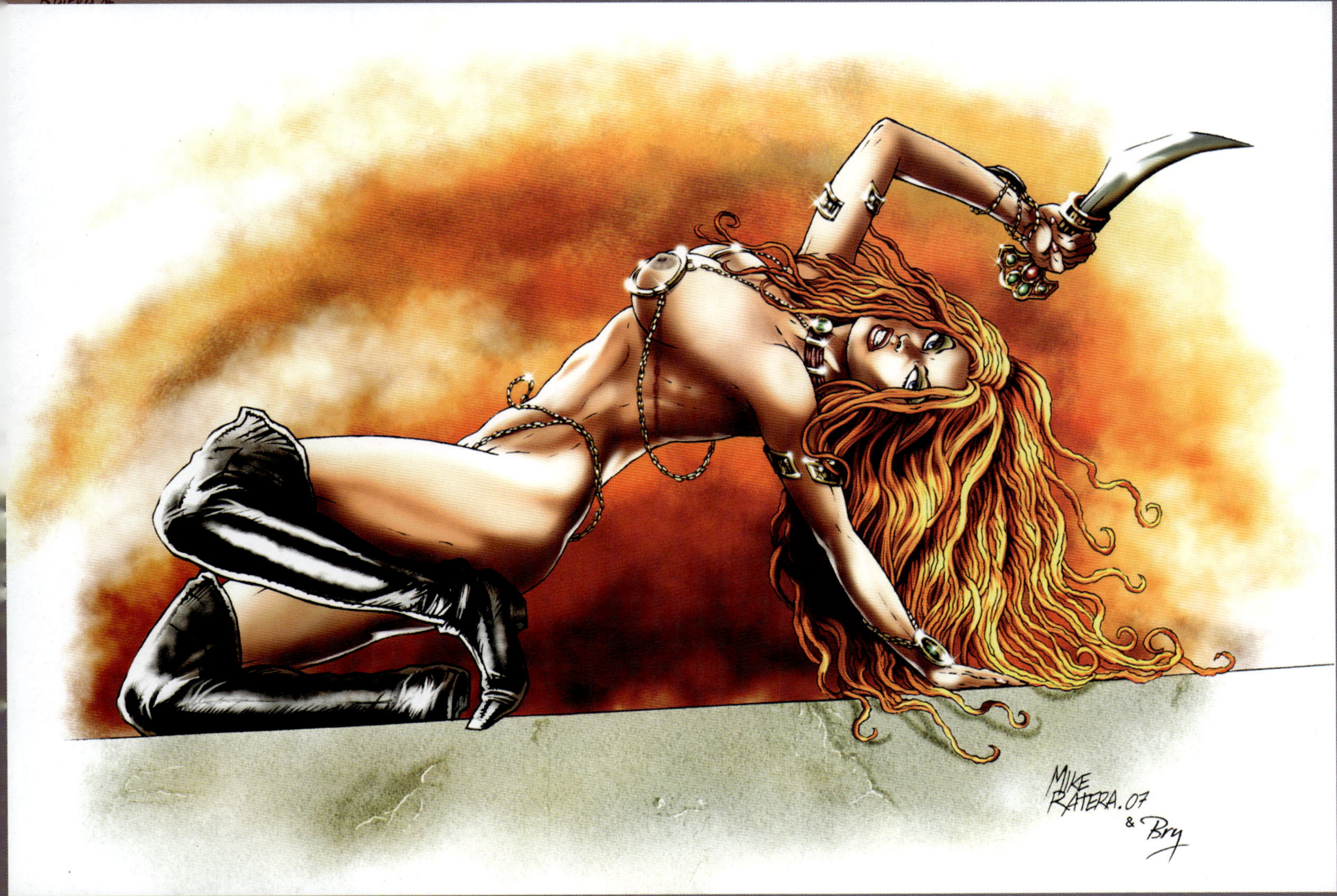
MIKE RATERA.07
& Bry

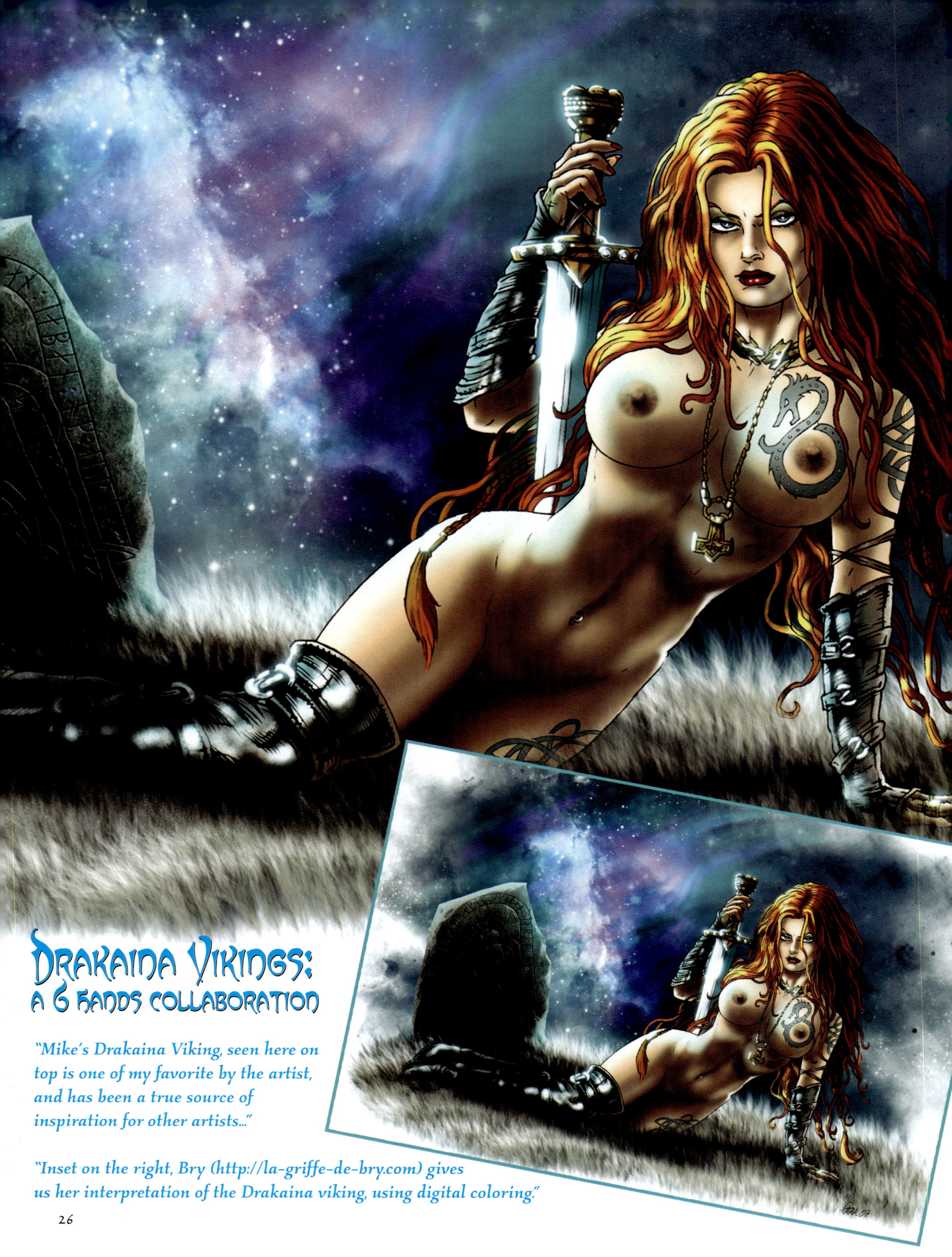

"Mike's Drakaina Viking, seen here on top is one of my favorite by the artist, and has been a true source of inspiration for other artists..."

"Inset on the right, Bry (http://la-griffe-de-bry.com) gives us her interpretation of the Drakaina viking, using digital coloring."

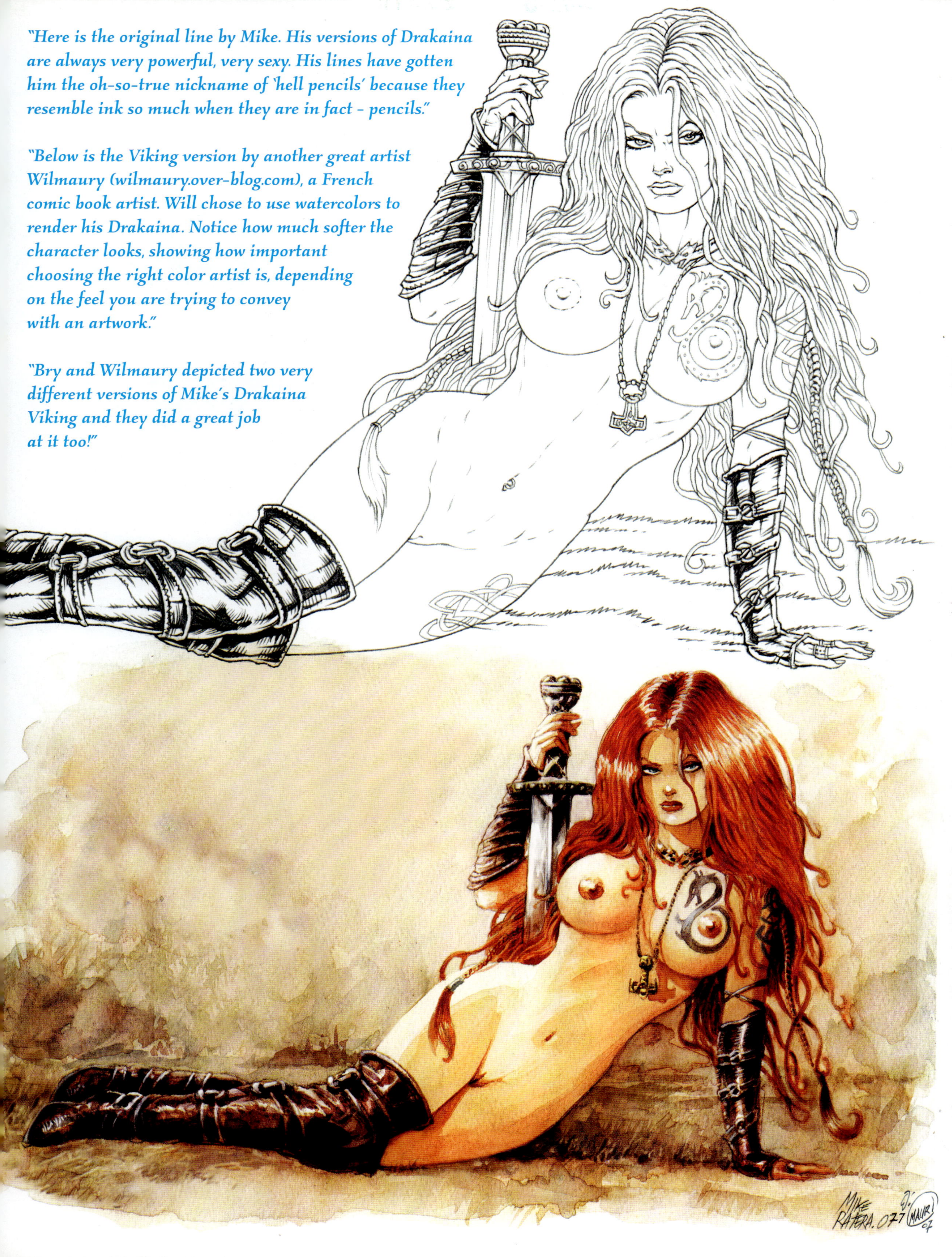

"Here is the original line by Mike. His versions of Drakaina are always very powerful, very sexy. His lines have gotten him the oh-so-true nickname of 'hell pencils' because they resemble ink so much when they are in fact - pencils."

"Below is the Viking version by another great artist Wilmaury (wilmaury.over-blog.com), a French comic book artist. Will chose to use watercolors to render his Drakaina. Notice how much softer the character looks, showing how important choosing the right color artist is, depending on the feel you are trying to convey with an artwork."

"Bry and Wilmaury depicted two very different versions of Mike's Drakaina Viking and they did a great job at it too!"

Each has its place
to do its deed
The flash of the sword
with its deadly speed

Dark angel cowers
to the blinding light
as white angel rules
with such regal right

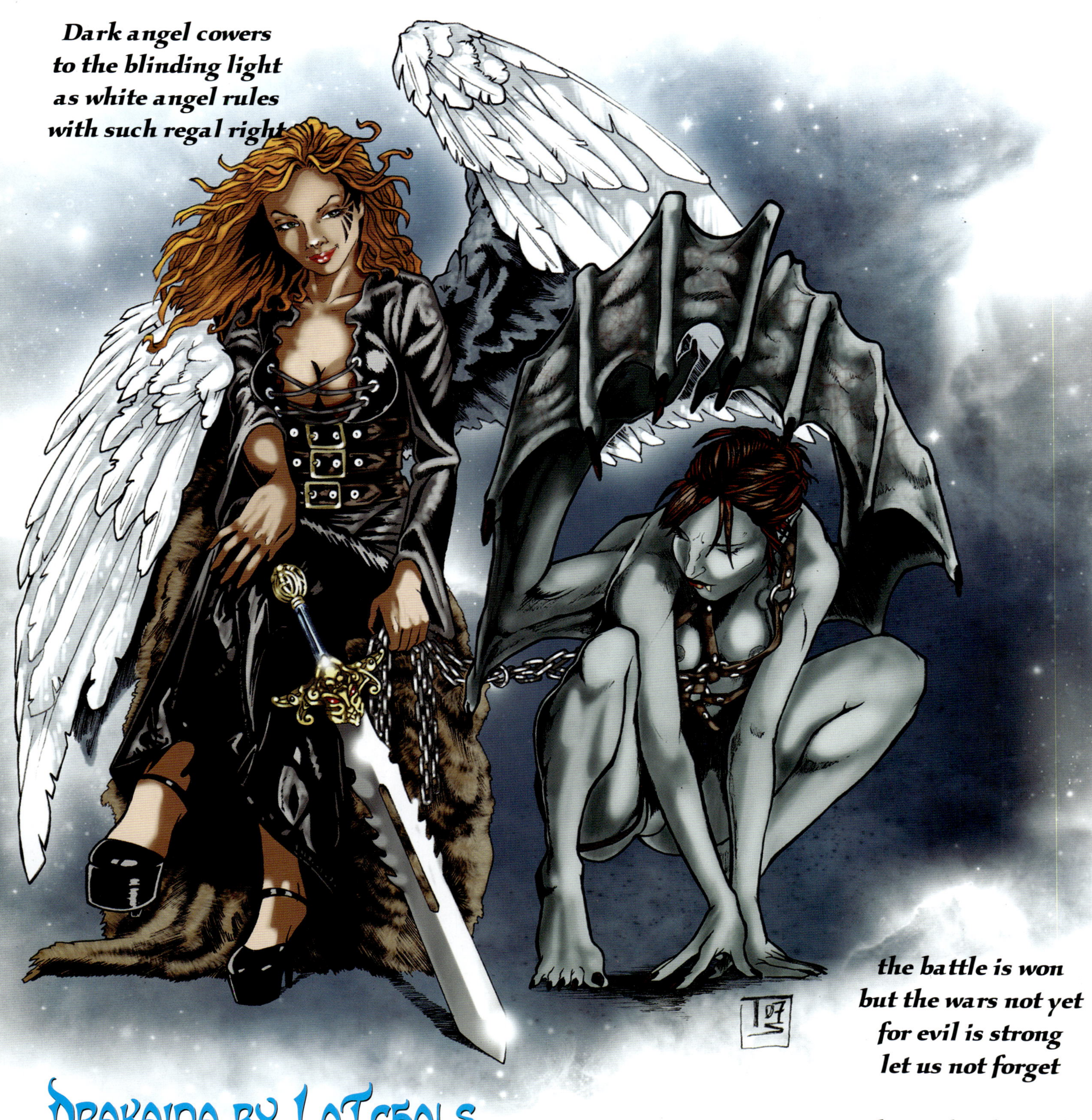

the battle is won
but the wars not yet
for evil is strong
let us not forget

chained to her side
in victory she stands
good has succeeded
and evil is banned

Drakaina by Latchals

Poem by Wayne Motherway
http://www.myspace.com/wayne_motherway

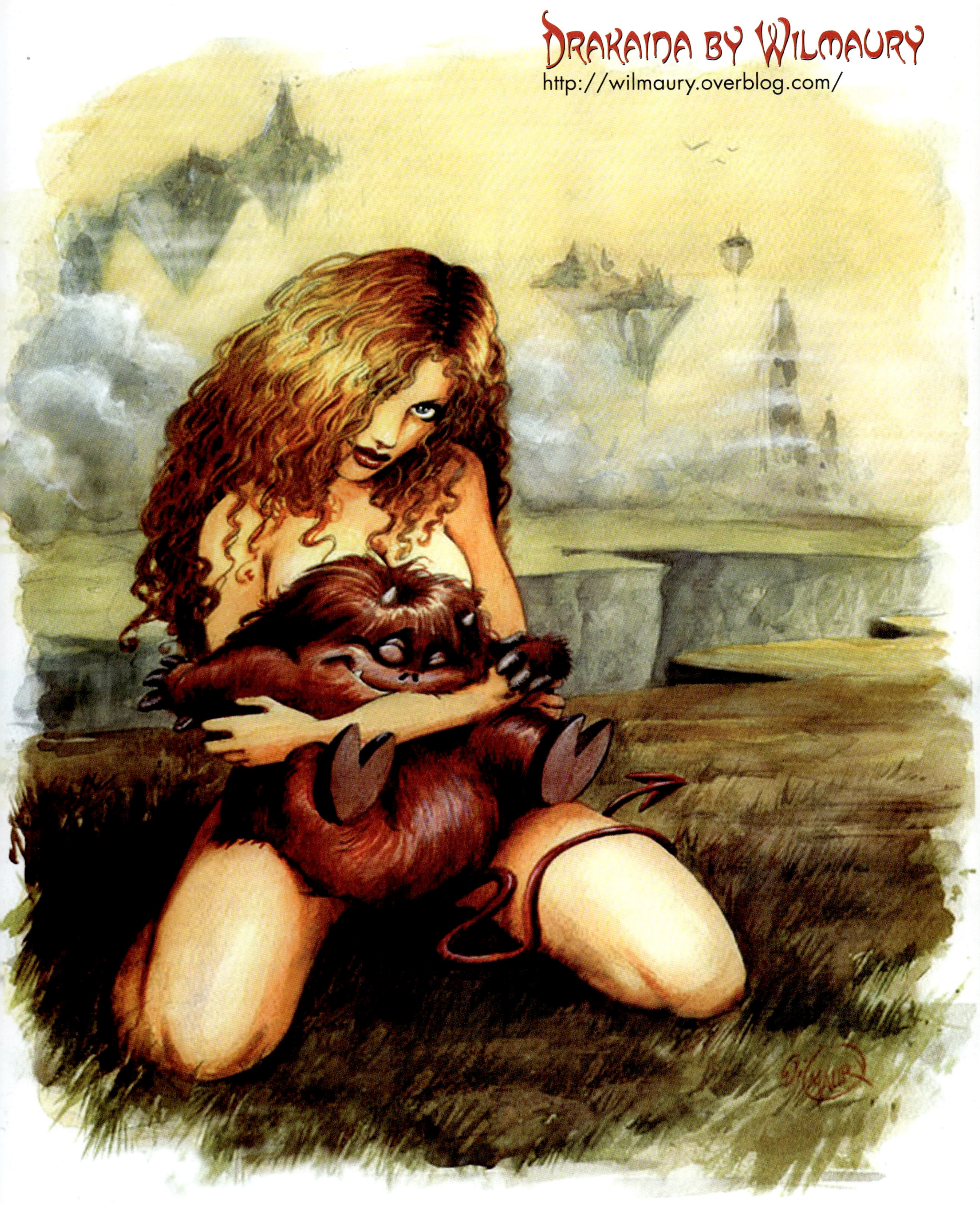

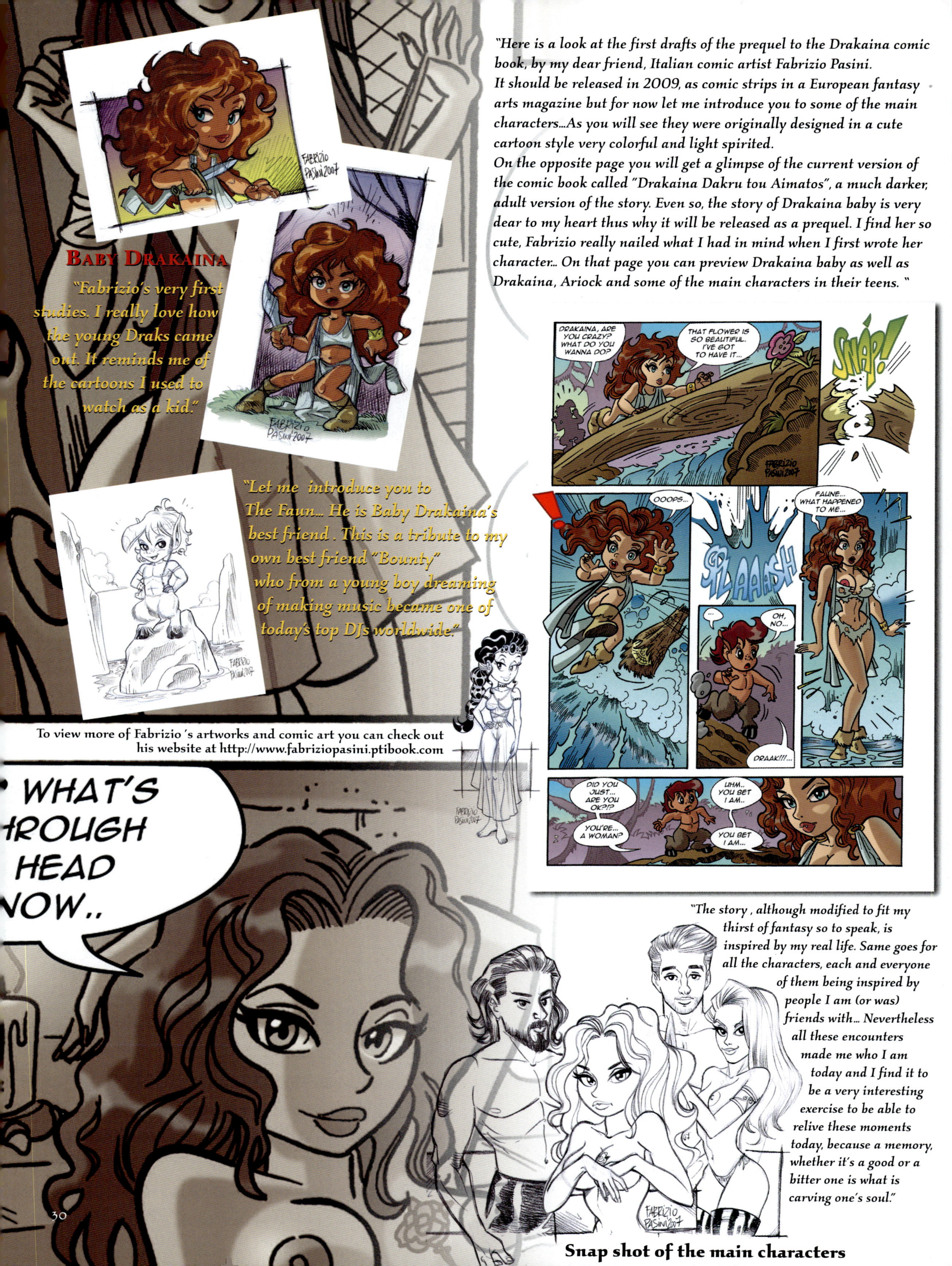

"Here is a look at the first drafts of the prequel to the Drakaina comic book, by my dear friend, Italian comic artist Fabrizio Pasini.
It should be released in 2009, as comic strips in a European fantasy arts magazine but for now let me introduce you to some of the main characters...As you will see they were originally designed in a cute cartoon style very colorful and light spirited.
On the opposite page you will get a glimpse of the current version of the comic book called "Drakaina Dakru tou Aimatos", a much darker, adult version of the story. Even so, the story of Drakaina baby is very dear to my heart thus why it will be released as a prequel. I find her so cute, Fabrizio really nailed what I had in mind when I first wrote her character... On that page you can preview Drakaina baby as well as Drakaina, Ariock and some of the main characters in their teens. "

Baby Drakaina

"Fabrizio's very first studies. I really love how the young Draks came out. It reminds me of the cartoons I used to watch as a kid."

"Let me introduce you to The Faun... He is Baby Drakaina's best friend . This is a tribute to my own best friend "Bounty" who from a young boy dreaming of making music became one of today's top DJs worldwide."

To view more of Fabrizio 's artworks and comic art you can check out his website at http://www.fabriziopasini.ptibook.com

"The story , although modified to fit my thirst of fantasy so to speak, is inspired by my real life. Same goes for all the characters, each and everyone of them being inspired by people I am (or was) friends with... Nevertheless all these encounters made me who I am today and I find it to be a very interesting exercise to be able to relive these moments today, because a memory, whether it's a good or a bitter one is what is carving one's soul."

Snap shot of the main characters

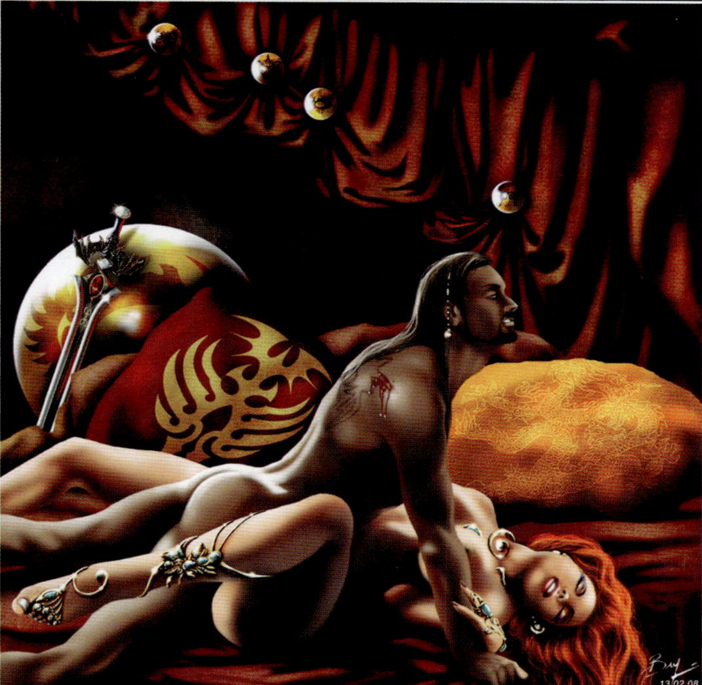

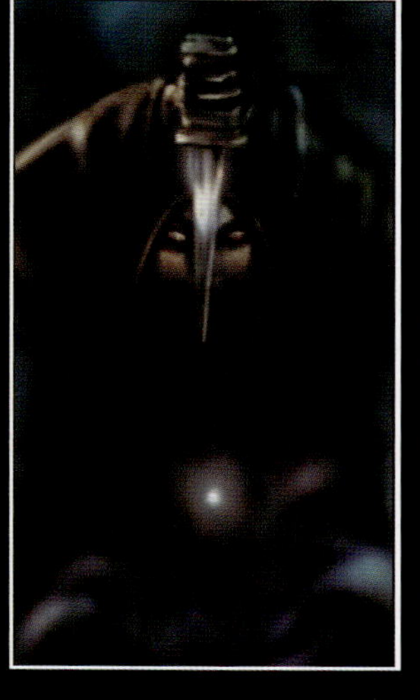

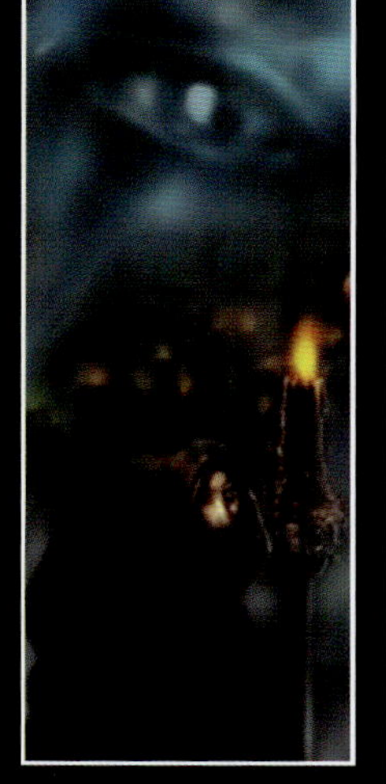

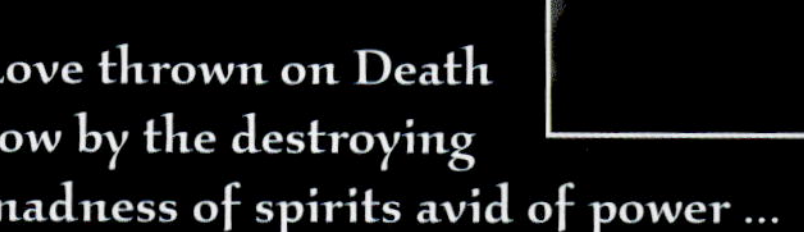

She is Drakaina, daughter of Drakonis, the primordial dragon and Gaia, mother nature. He is Ariock, son of Hecate, goddess of the night ruling the underworld. These two should have never met and yet…

Their love is legendary, breaking all the rules, sharing a forbidden happiness in spite of their differences.

But it was a long time ago…

Love thrown on Death row by the destroying madness of spirits avid of power …

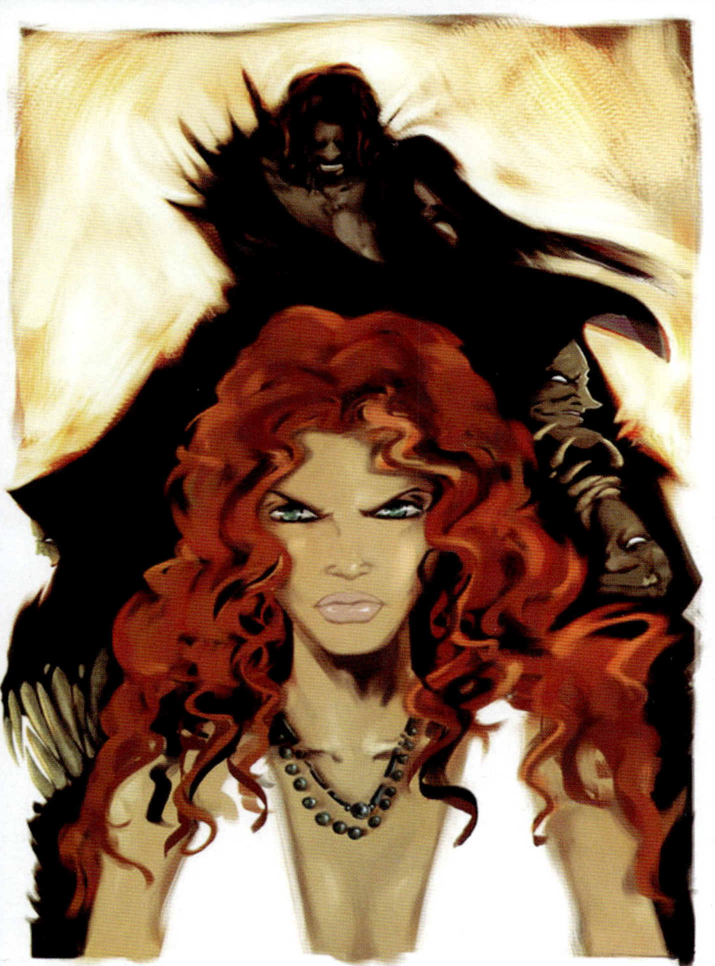

Today nature took back its rights, and they fight with same passion that they once shared…

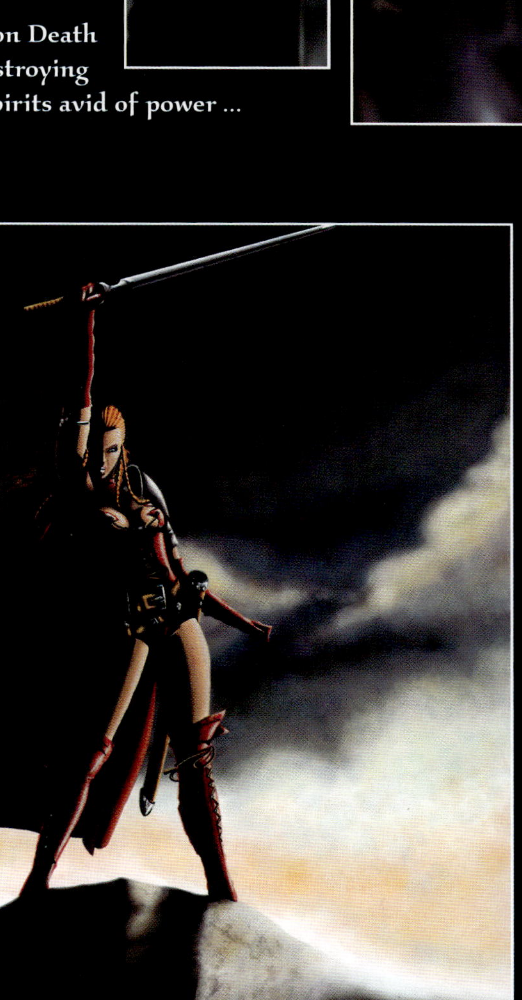

From this tearing fight only one will rise …

Drakaina, The Graphic Novel

by various artists

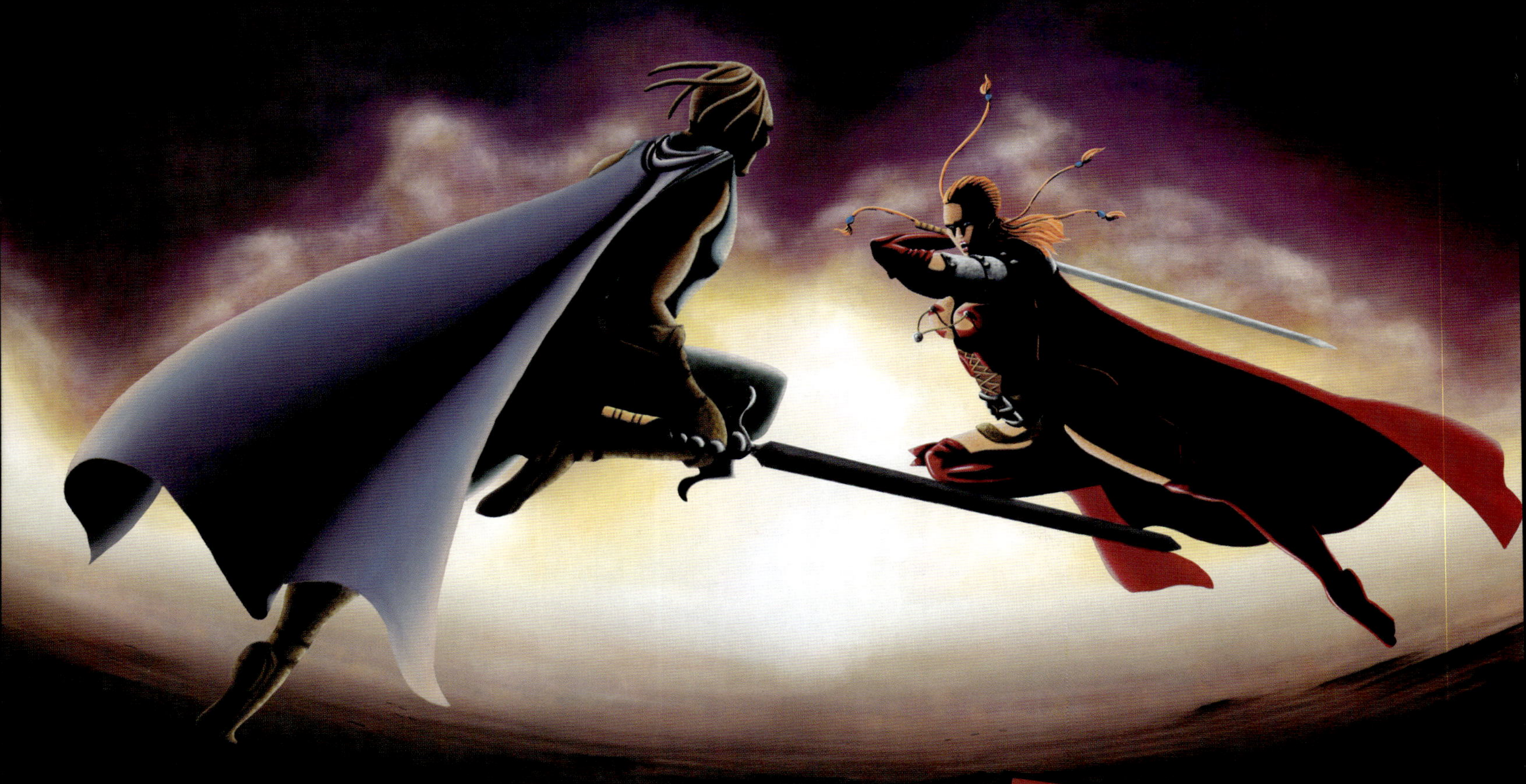

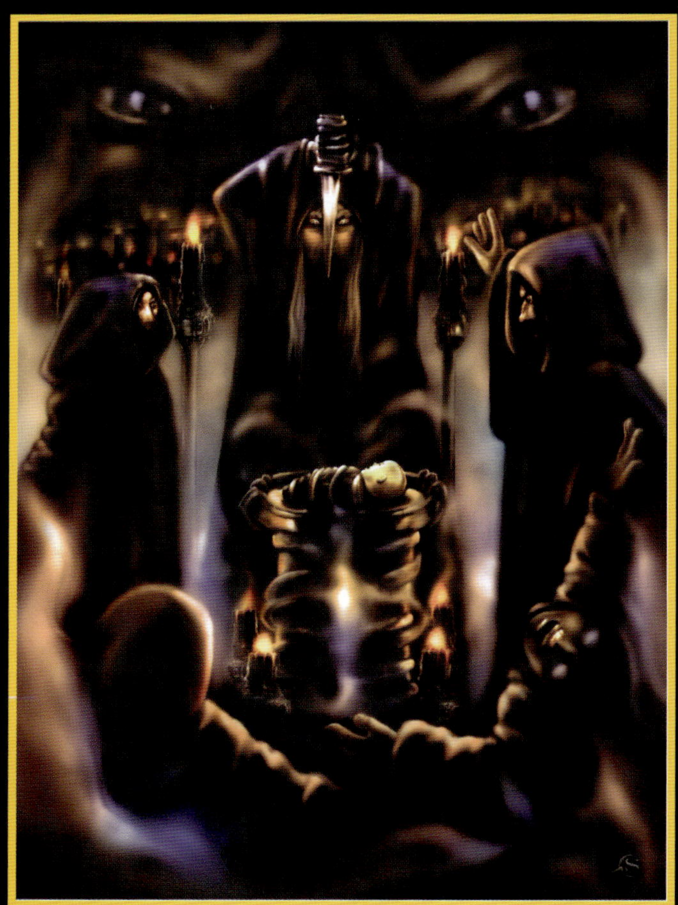

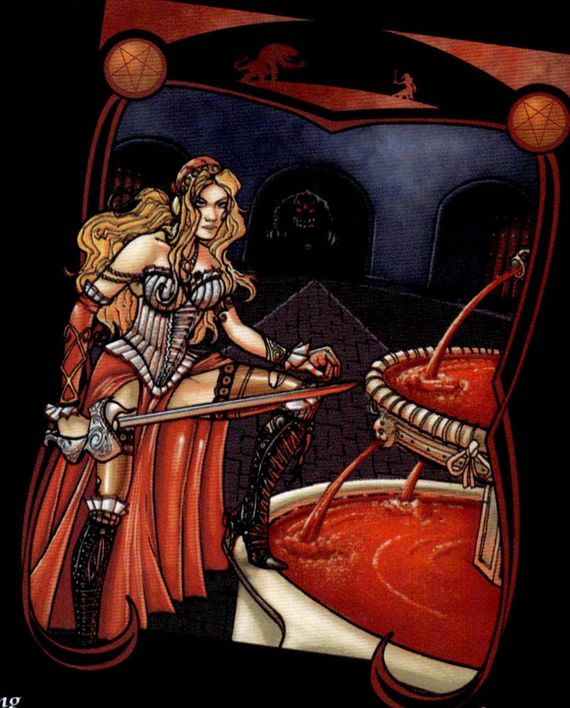

"As you can
see, the upcoming
Drakaina graphic novel has already inspired a
panel of various artists worldwide. On both this page and the previous one,
the artworks are made by the Baywin.net members
 (Orejona (http://www.la-griffe-de-Bry.com), Sadelegy ,
Osh (http://planeted.canalblog.com/), Cyrilou (http://20six.fr/cyrilou)
and Maddog (http://www.madd-og.com/))."

"Following page, Ariock surprised me with the concept/cover art for the
second part of the Drakaina story, which will be called 'Redemption'"

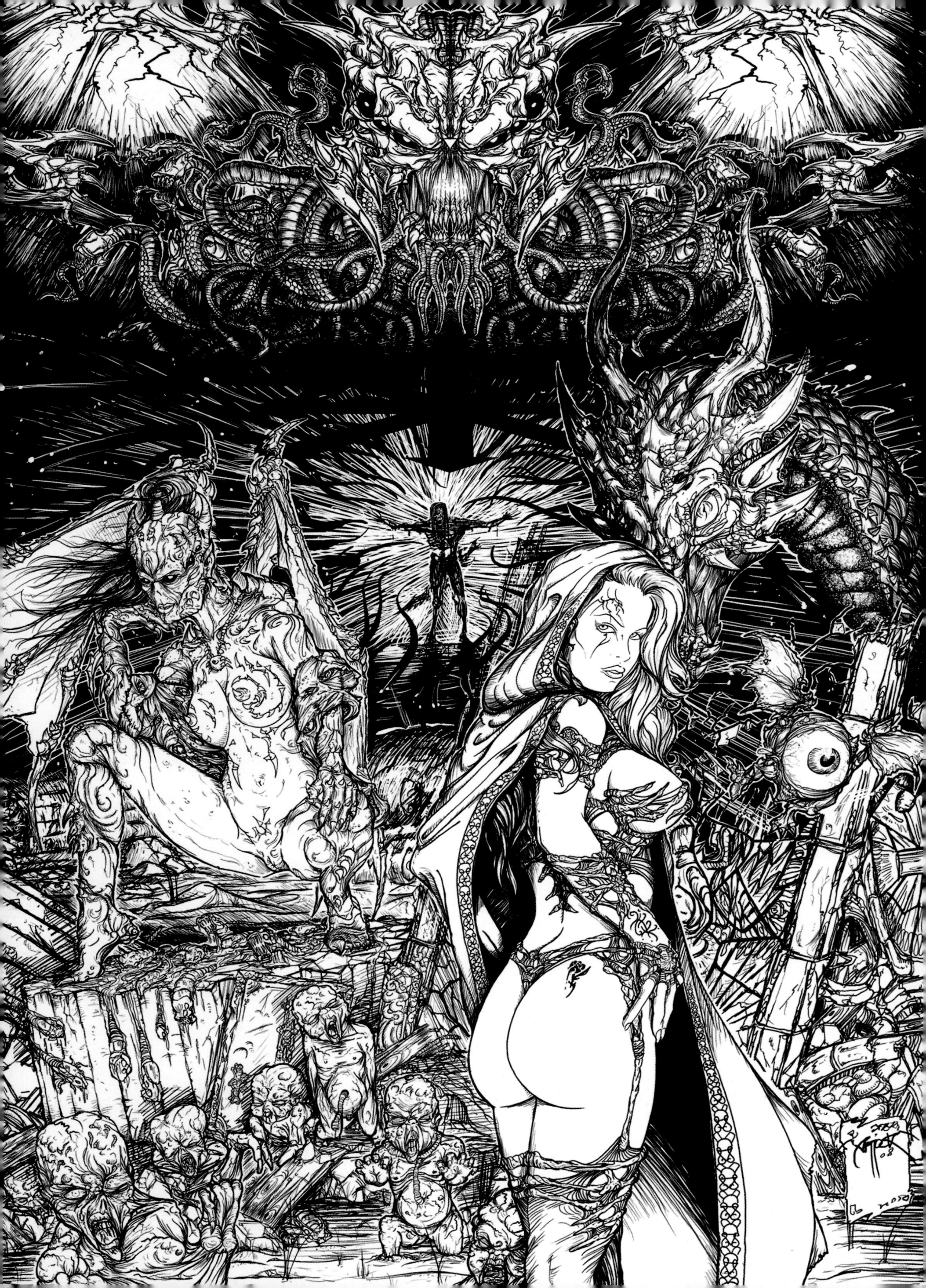

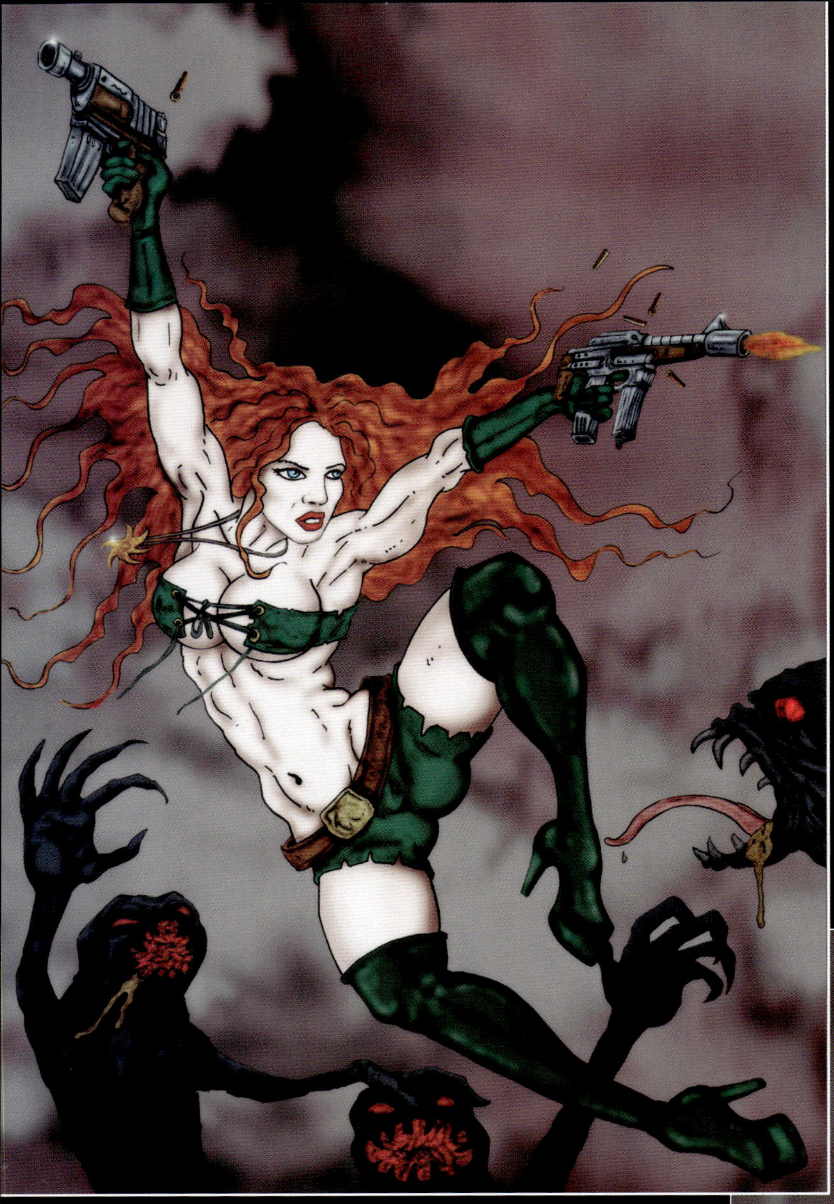

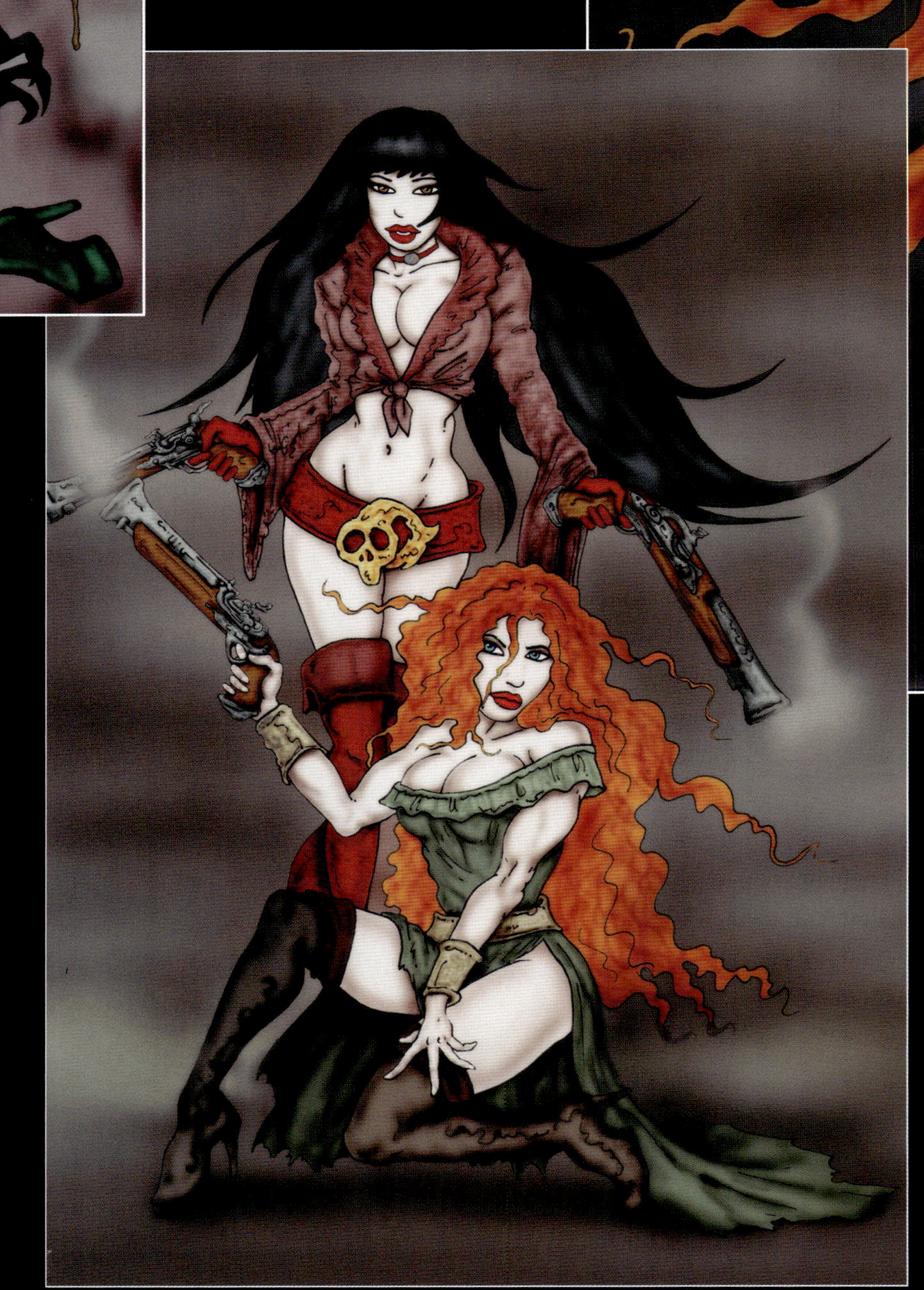

"The sexy brunette with me on the drawings is Tancrède's lovely wife Ijsselina, who started to take interest in posing for artists too a few months ago."

"Ijsselina and I also share a deep passion for animal rights and are both fighting hard for animals to have a better life."

"I can't say much for now but you should here more about us and our fight for animals pretty soon..."

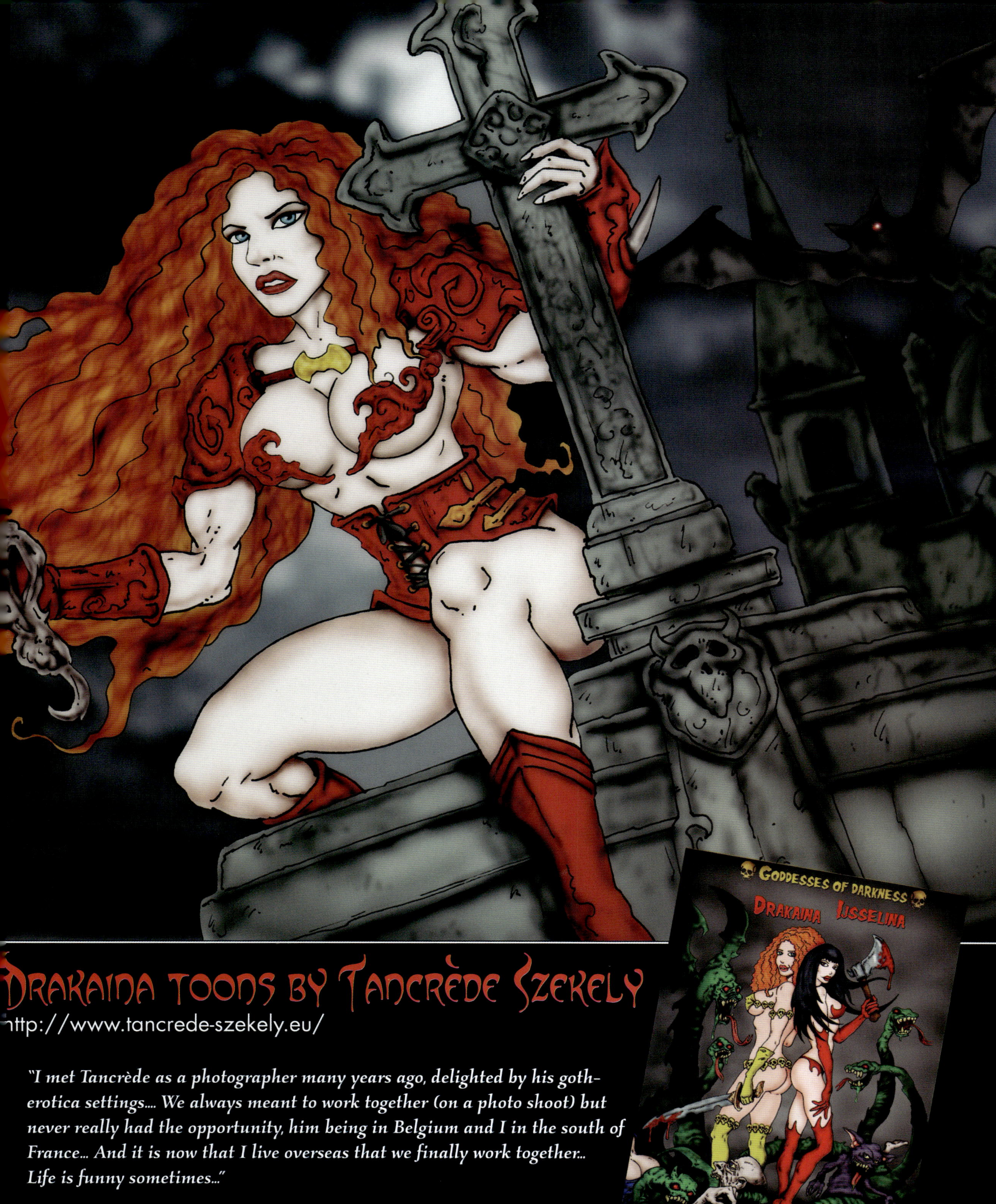

Drakaina toons by Tancrède Szekely

http://www.tancrede-szekely.eu/

"I met Tancrède as a photographer many years ago, delighted by his goth-erotica settings.... We always meant to work together (on a photo shoot) but never really had the opportunity, him being in Belgium and I in the south of France... And it is now that I live overseas that we finally work together... Life is funny sometimes..."

On both pages are toon versions of Drakaina by Tancrède, master of erotic photography now toon artist!

When I heard that Drakaina was looking for artists and paintings to include in her upcoming art-book I asked her to be part of the crew immediately.

Once I knew that I'll be in the book I went enthusiast and after the completion of the job I must affirm that Drakaina is not only a very beautiful woman and an amazing model but she's also a very professional person which is a pleasure to work with.

Her beautiful body and her curly, long, red hairs are a wonderful subject to paint and for this piece my idea was that her immortal beautiful came from her relation with the Master of Time who's been depicted behind her.

Pierre Luigi A.

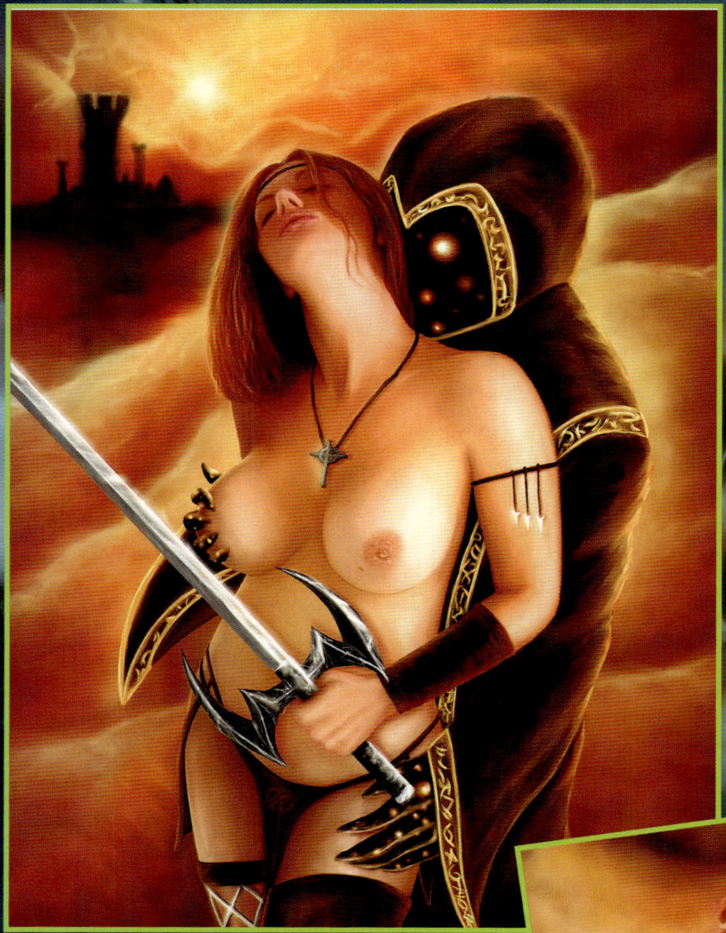

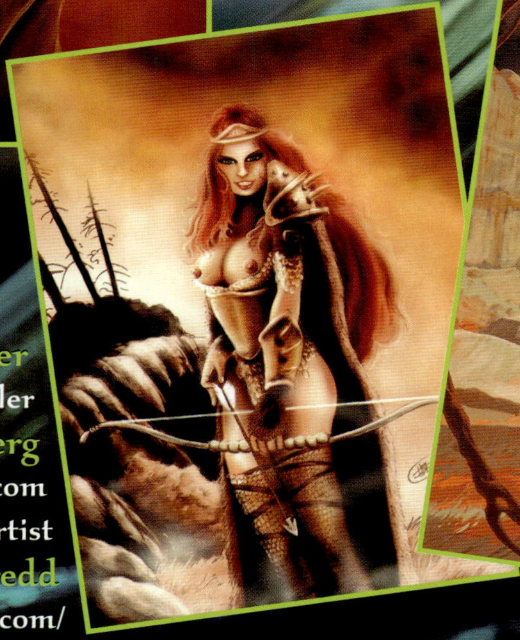

Drakaina by Pascal Isac
http://pascal.izac.free.fr/

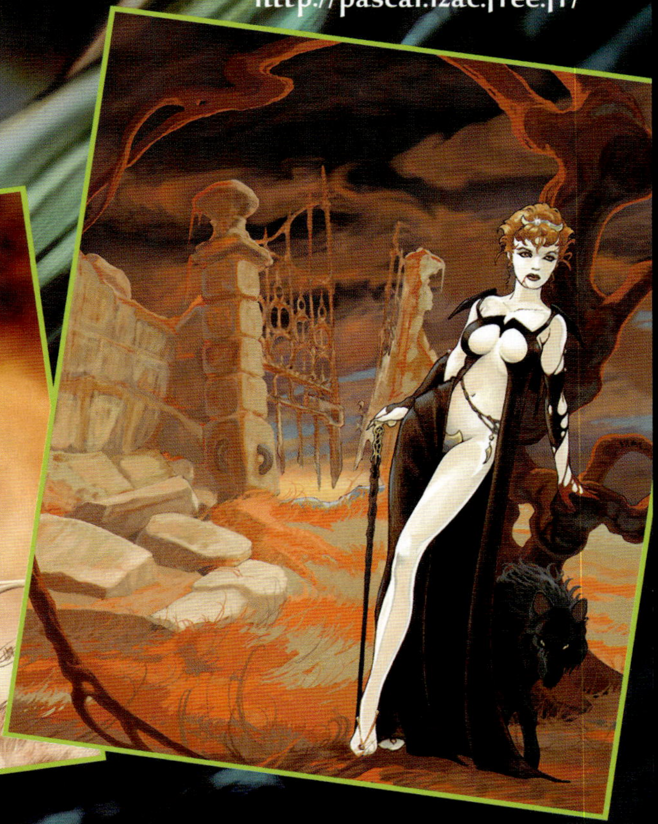

Drakaina by
Pierre Luigi Abbodanza
http://www.abboart.com/

The Drakaina Archer
is a cross collaboration between penciler
Deberg
http://deberg.canalblog.com
and color artist
Fredd
http://www.fredd-illustrations.com/

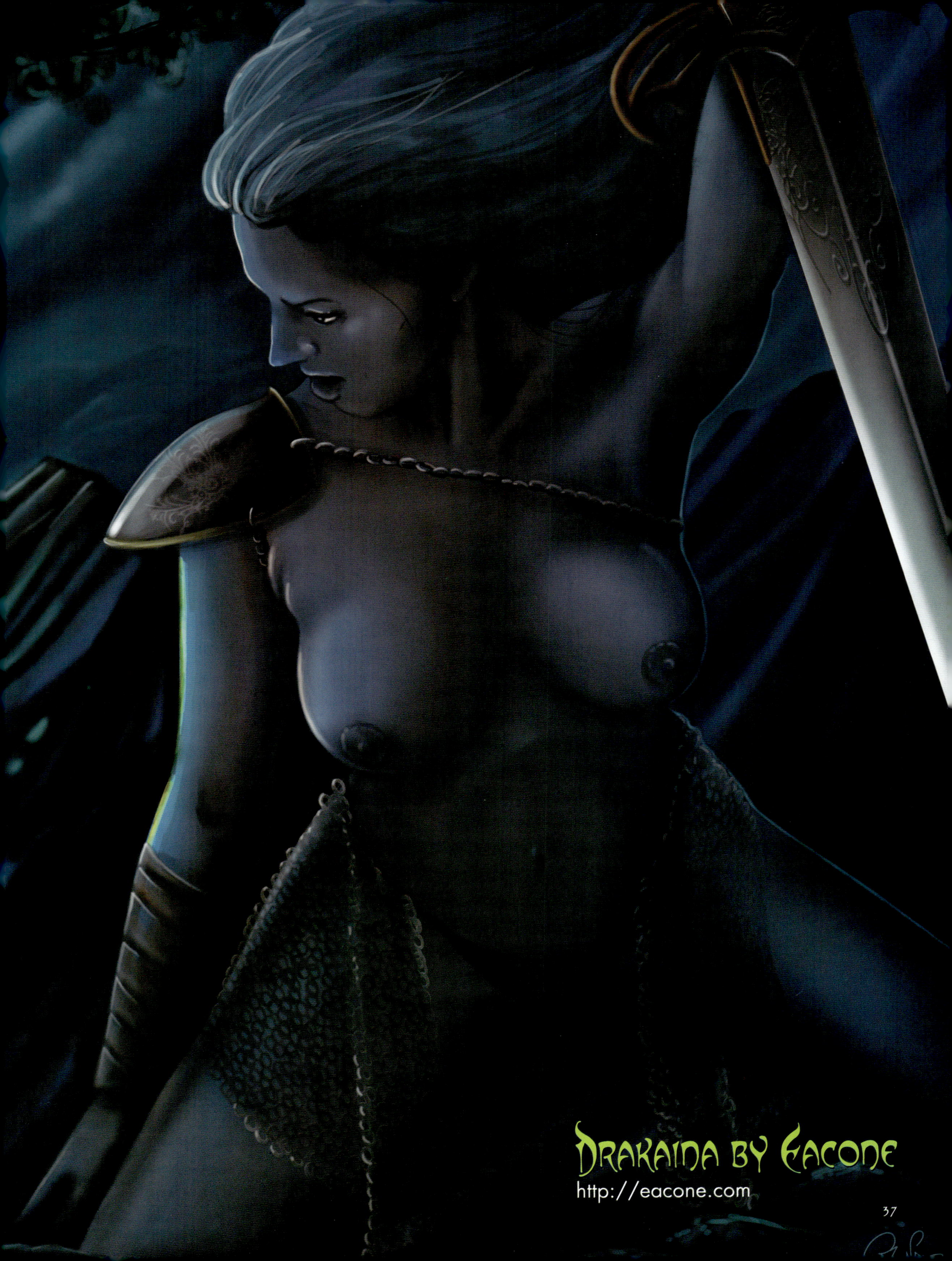

Drakaina by Eacone
http://eacone.com

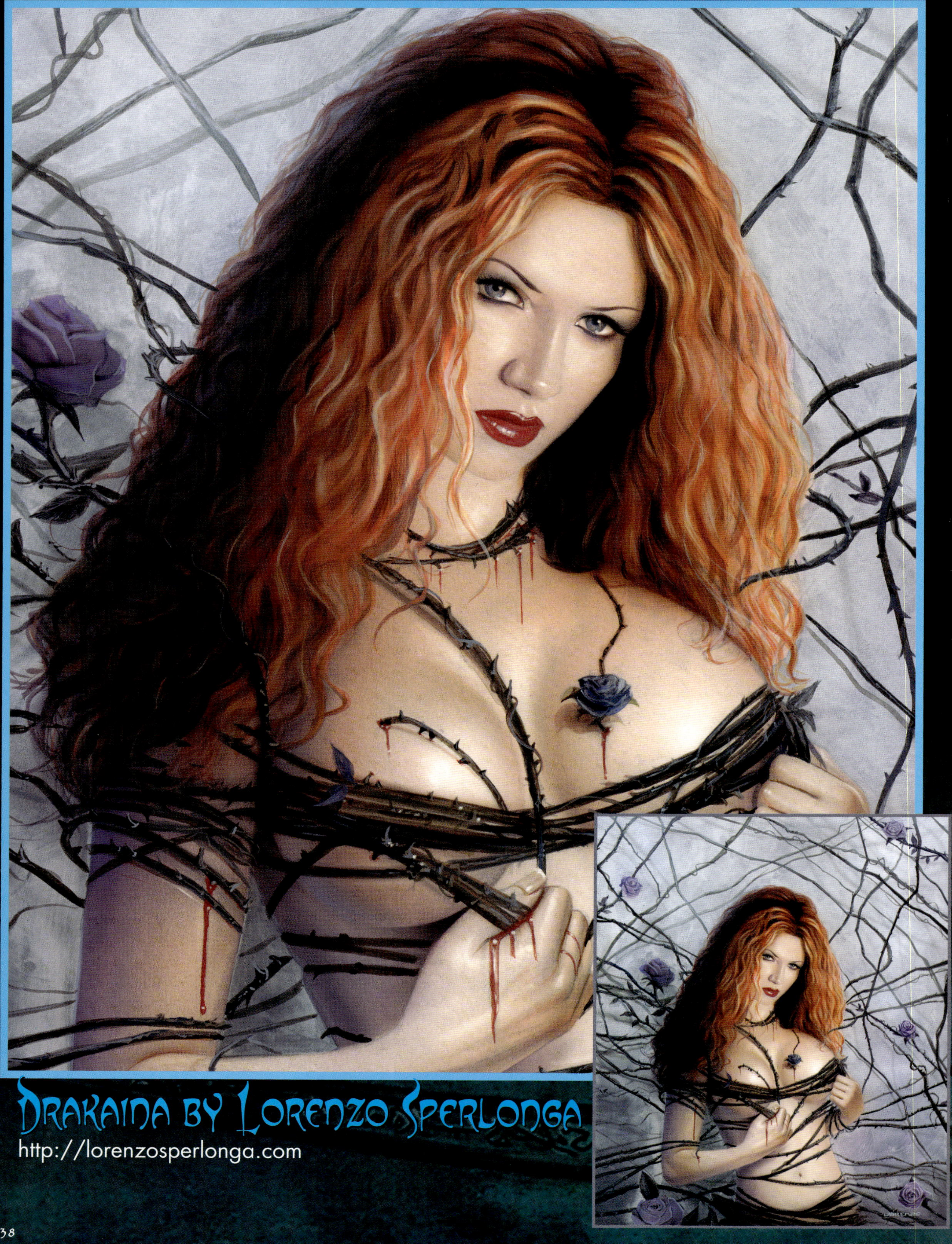

Drakaina by Lorenzo Sperlonga
http://lorenzosperlonga.com

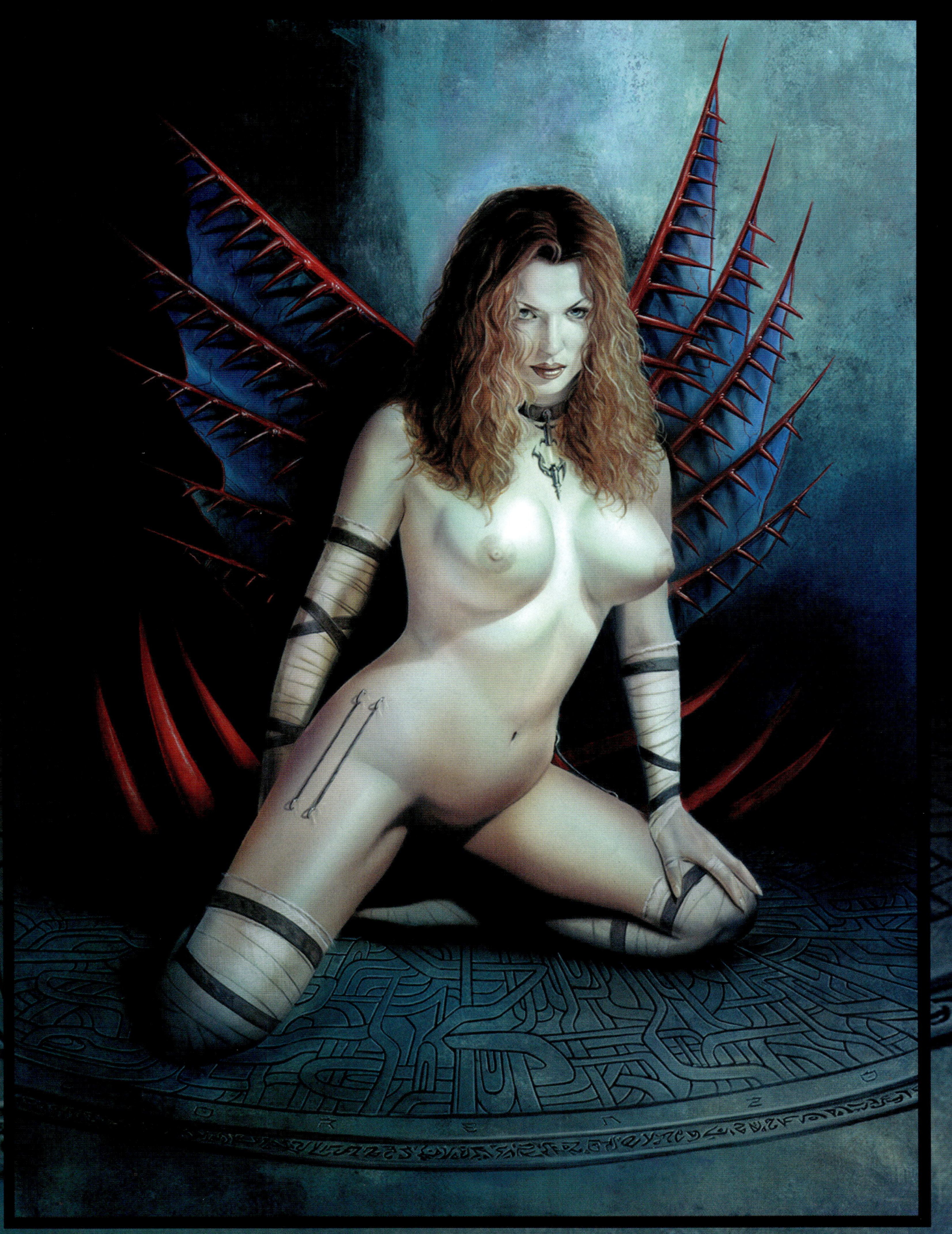

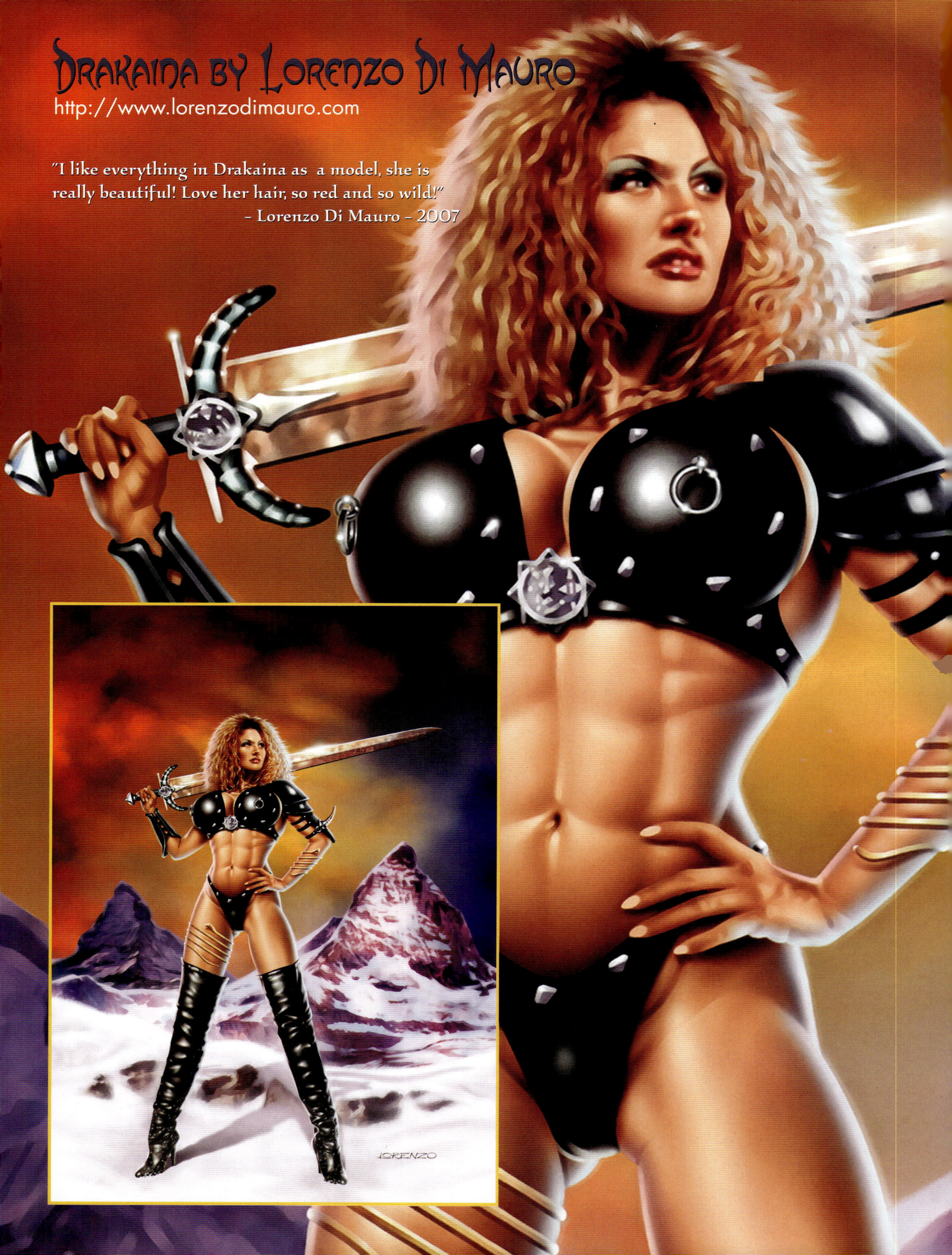

Drakaina by Lorenzo Di Mauro
http://www.lorenzodimauro.com
"I like everything in Drakaina as a model, she is really beautiful! Love her hair, so red and so wild!"
– Lorenzo Di Mauro – 2007
LORENZO

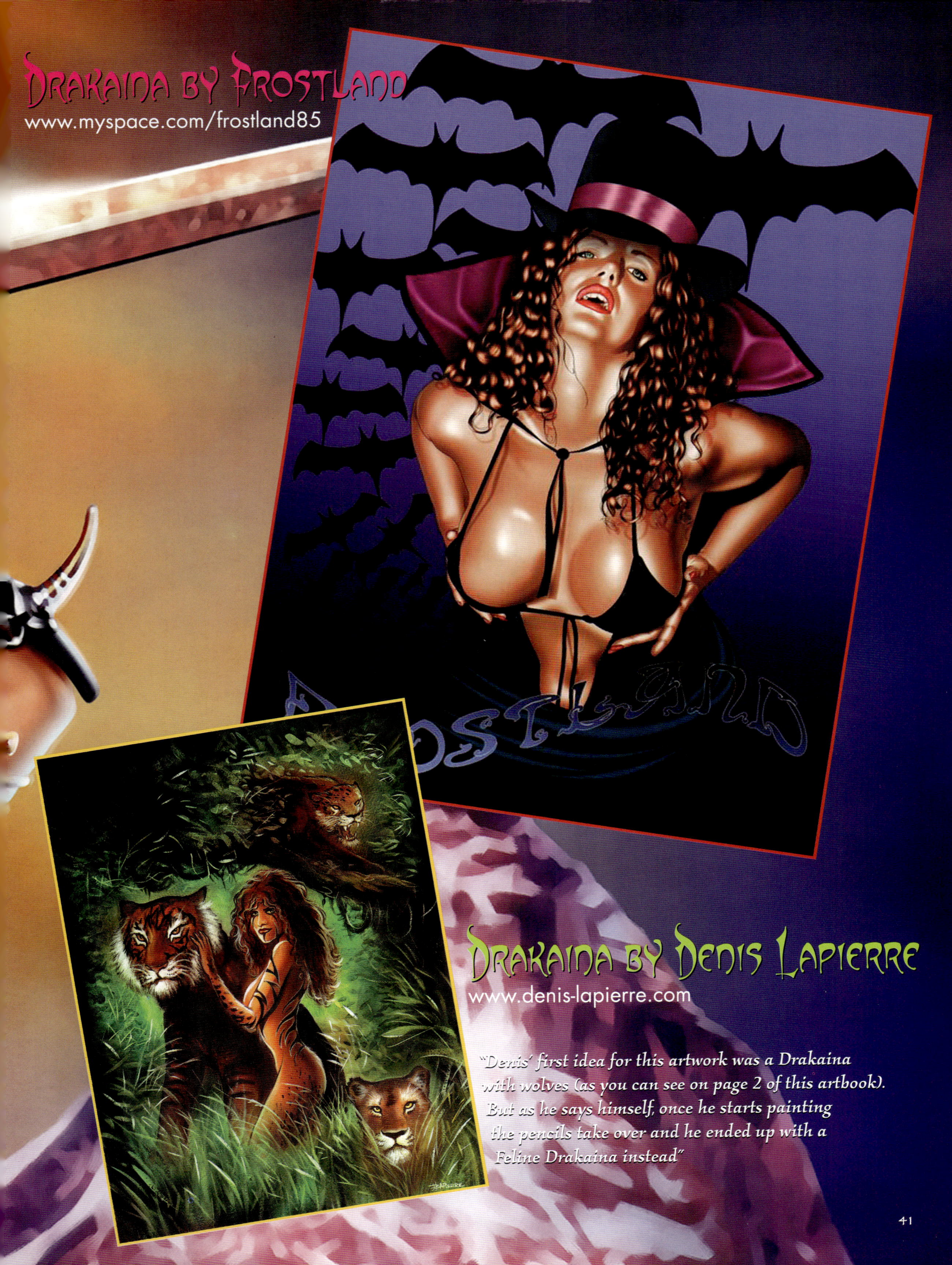
Drakaina by Frostland
www.myspace.com/frostland85
FROSTLAND
Drakaina by Denis Lapierre
www.denis-lapierre.com
"Denis' first idea for this artwork was a Drakaina
with wolves (as you can see on page 2 of this artbook).
But as he says himself, once he starts painting
the pencils take over and he ended up with a
Feline Drakaina instead"

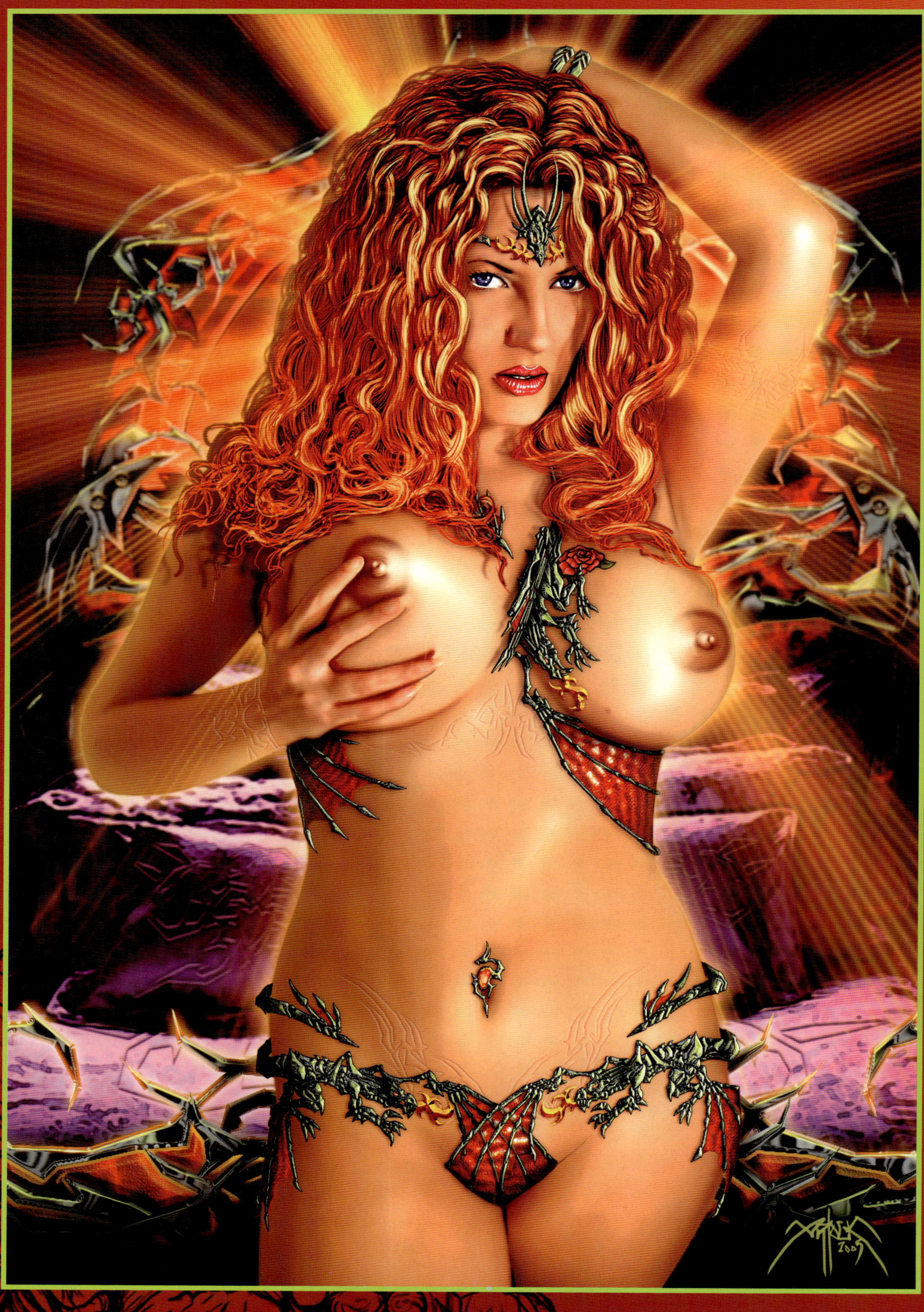

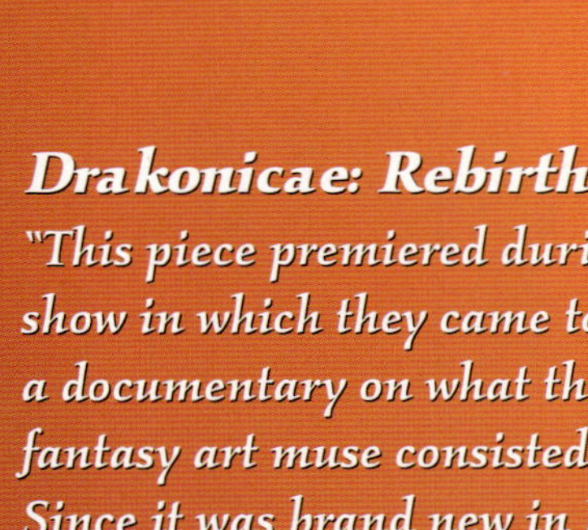

Drakonicae: Rebirth...

"This piece premiered during a French TV show in which they came to the house to do a documentary on what the life of a fantasy art muse consisted of.
Since it was brand new in France the producer of the show wanted to show the birth of an artwork from the original concept art, the photo shoot and the "construction" of the artwork. So they filmed Ariock's computer screen while he was painting and explaining what he was doing.

For some reason I never published this artwork on my website , which is kind of funny cuz I really like it..."

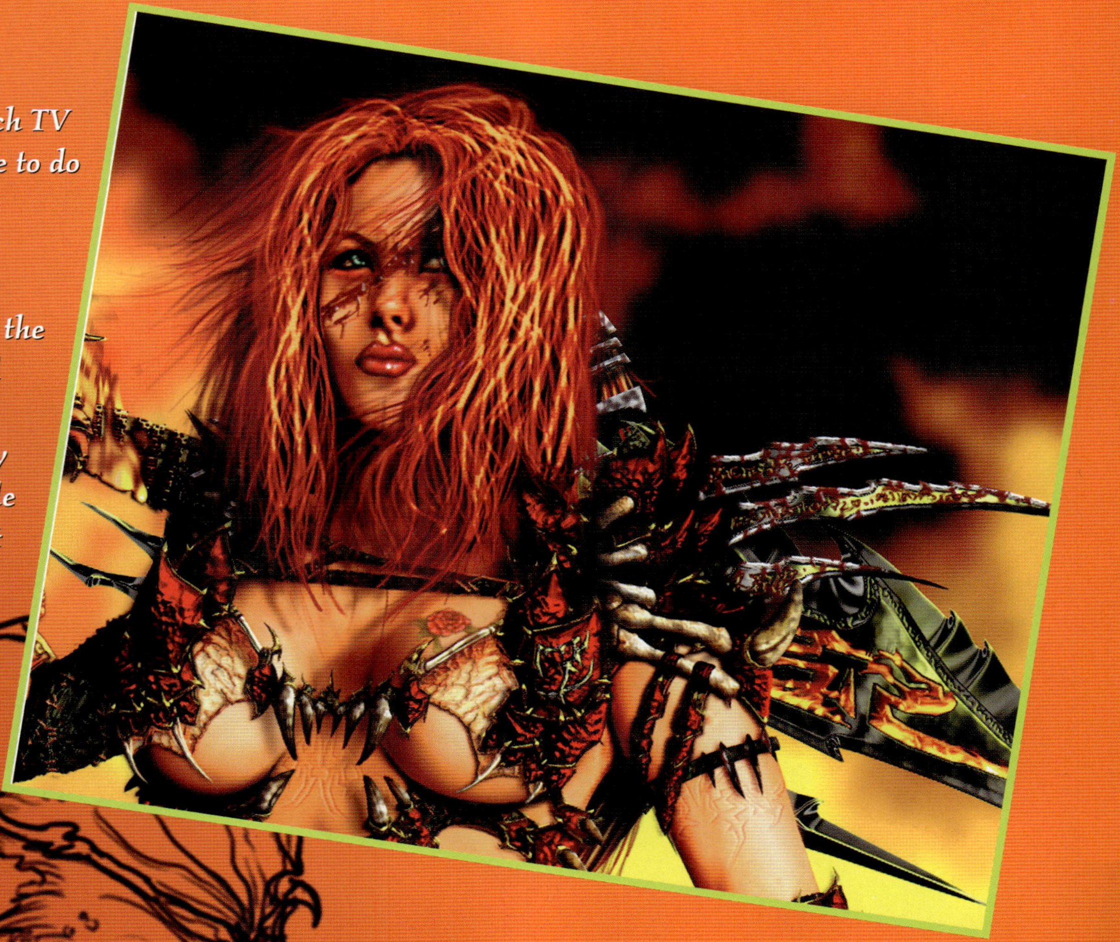

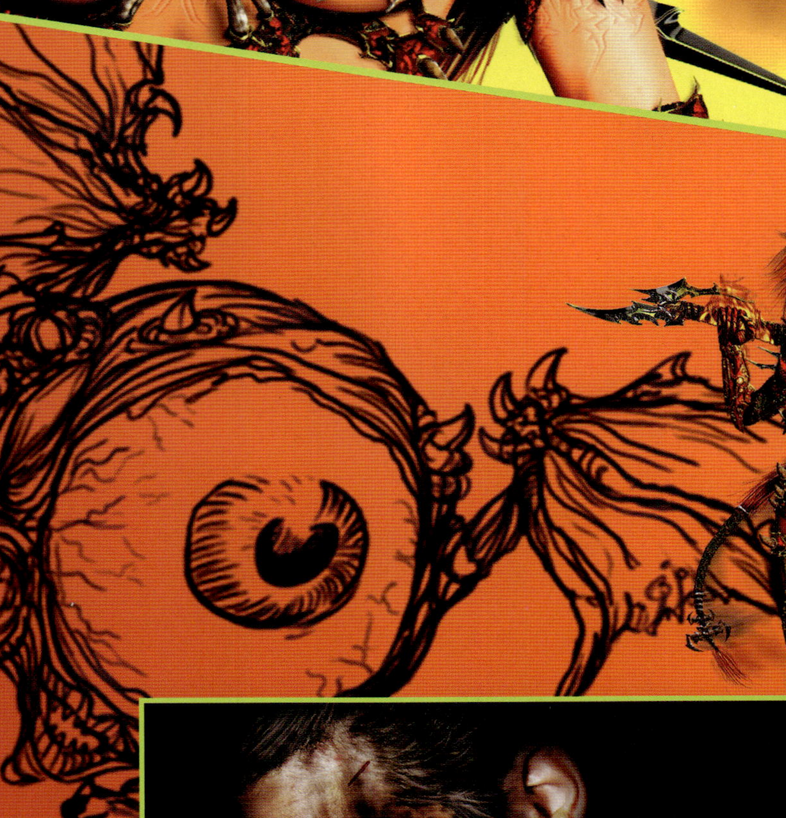

DRAKAINA BY ARIOCK

http://ariock.com

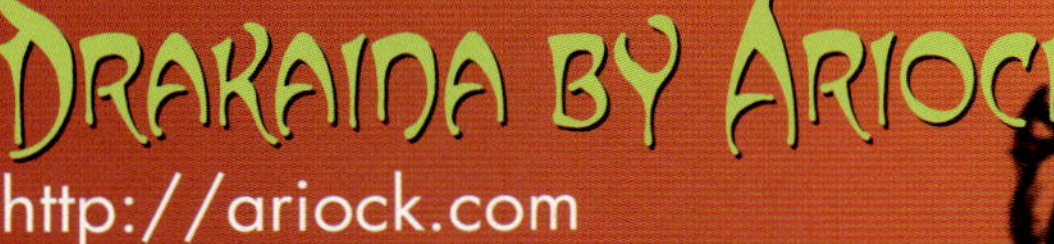

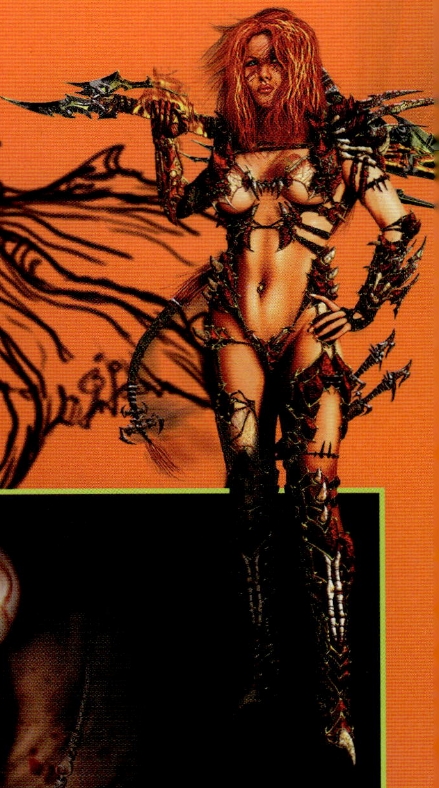

"Although we share the same passion for fantasy arts, Ariock and I have opposite tastes in the matter: when you look at a Drakaina painting, I like to think that it will make you dream... When Ariock creates a new artworks it's to reach out to your deepest nightmares...'

To the right is a self portrait of the artist, true to himself, as always....

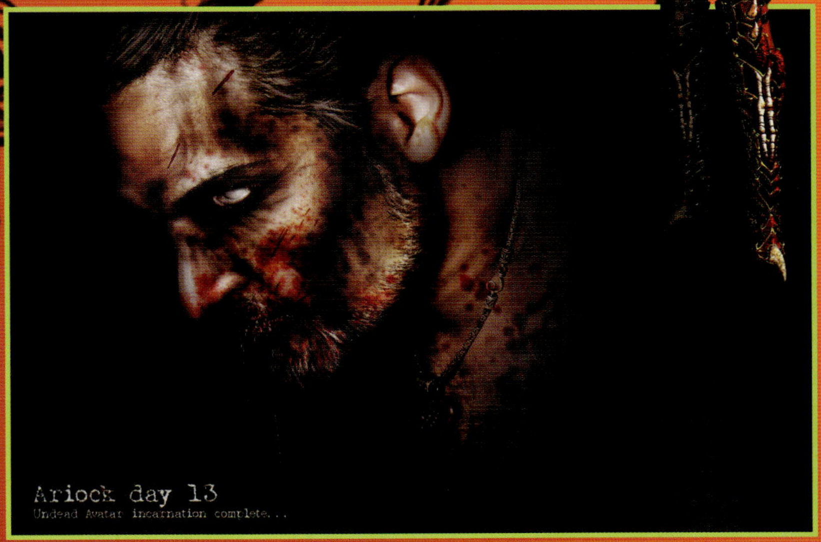

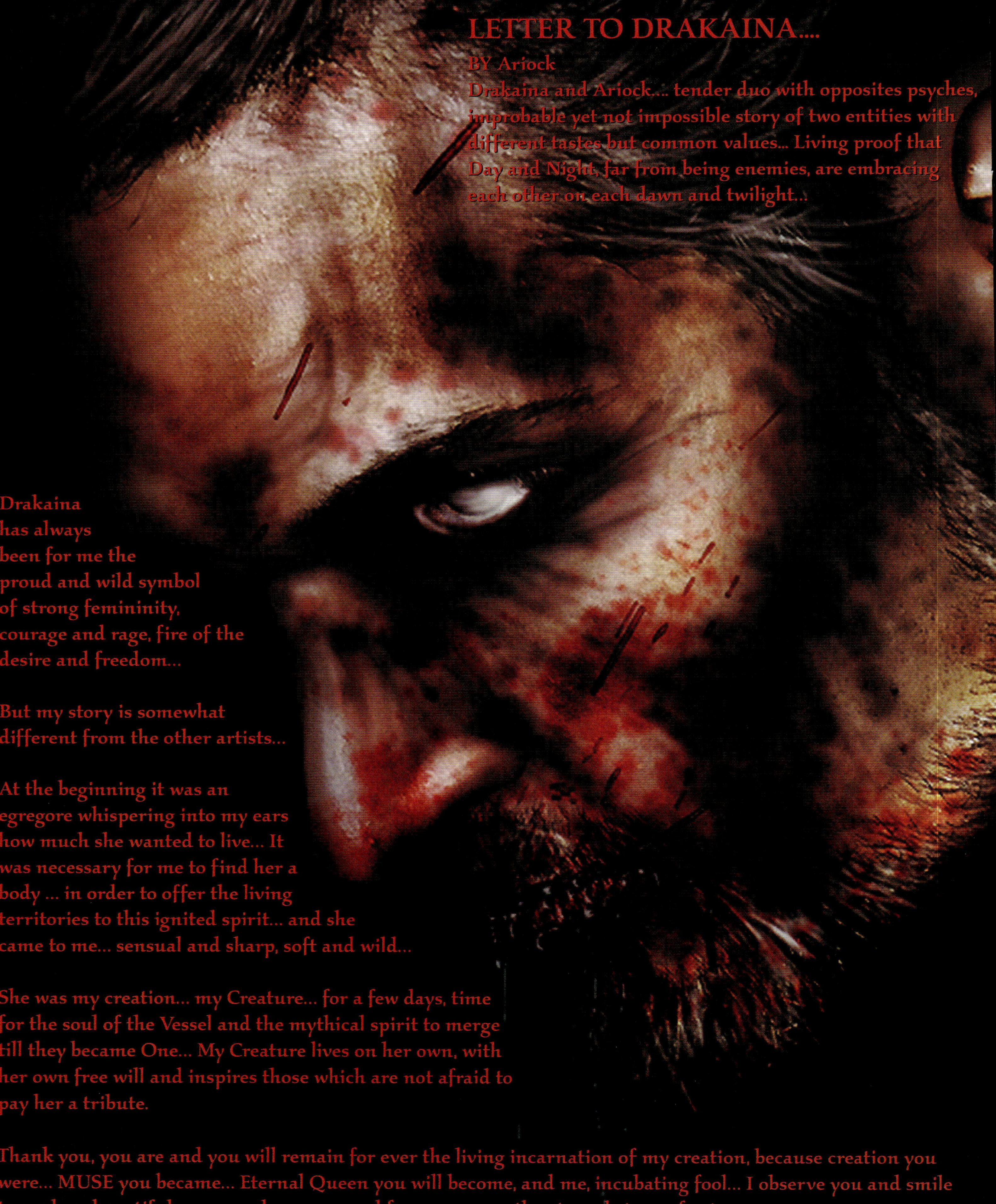

LETTER TO DRAKAINA....

BY Ariock

Drakaina and Ariock... tender duo with opposites psyches, improbable yet not impossible story of two entities with different tastes but common values... Living proof that Day and Night, far from being enemies, are embracing each other on each dawn and twilight...

Drakaina
has always
been for me the
proud and wild symbol
of strong femininity,
courage and rage, fire of the
desire and freedom...

But my story is somewhat
different from the other artists...

At the beginning it was an
egregore whispering into my ears
how much she wanted to live... It
was necessary for me to find her a
body ... in order to offer the living
territories to this ignited spirit... and she
came to me... sensual and sharp, soft and wild...

She was my creation... my Creature... for a few days, time
for the soul of the Vessel and the mythical spirit to merge
till they became One... My Creature lives on her own, with
her own free will and inspires those which are not afraid to
pay her a tribute.

Thank you, you are and you will remain for ever the living incarnation of my creation, because creation you
were... MUSE you became... Eternal Queen you will become, and me, incubating fool... I observe you and smile
to see how beautiful you are when your soul forever carves the eternal stone of arts.

My Child, my Queen, my Love, you were able to steal the shine of imagination and capture it in the jewels of
your beauty so that forever the artists continue to dream...

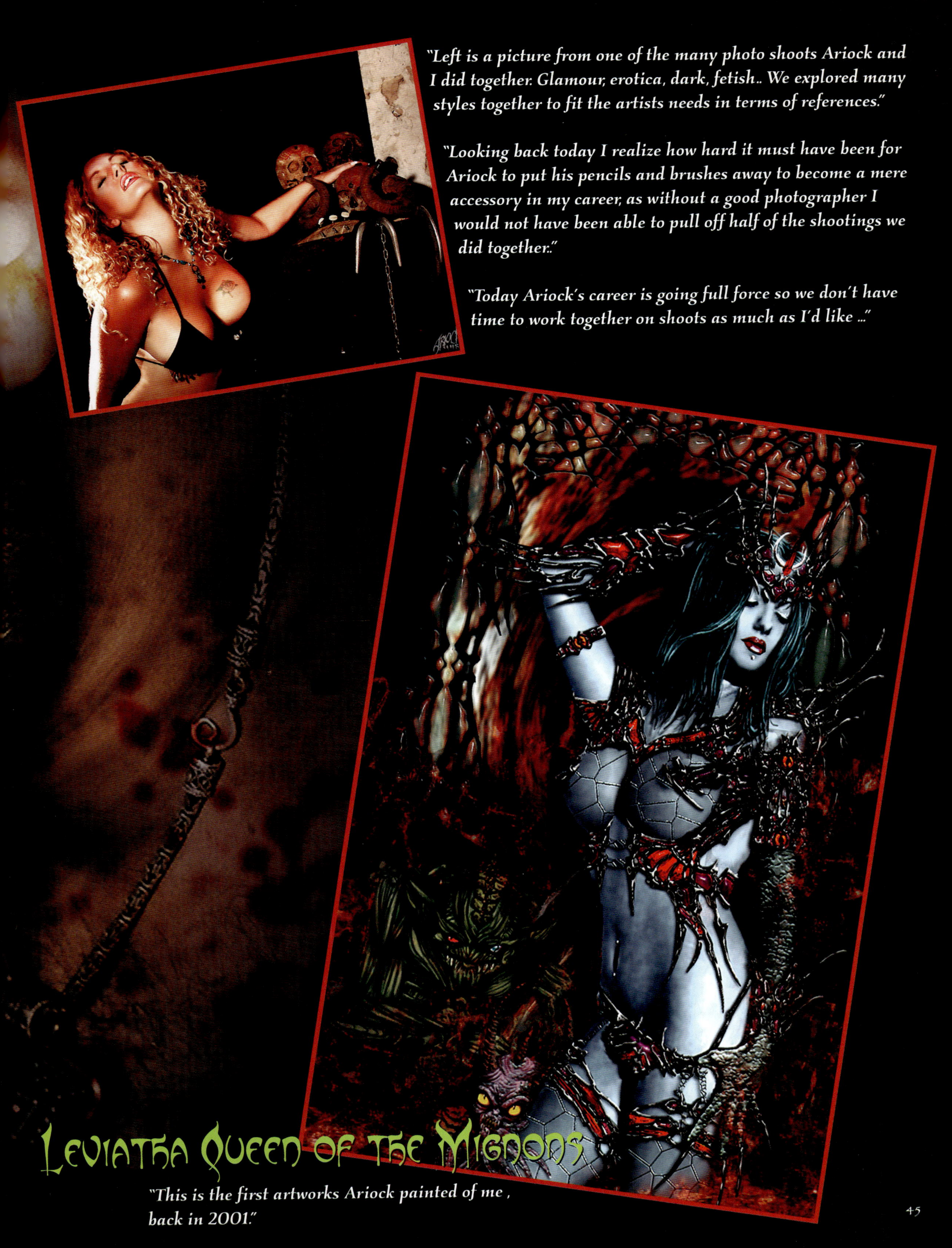

Leviatha Queen of the Mignons

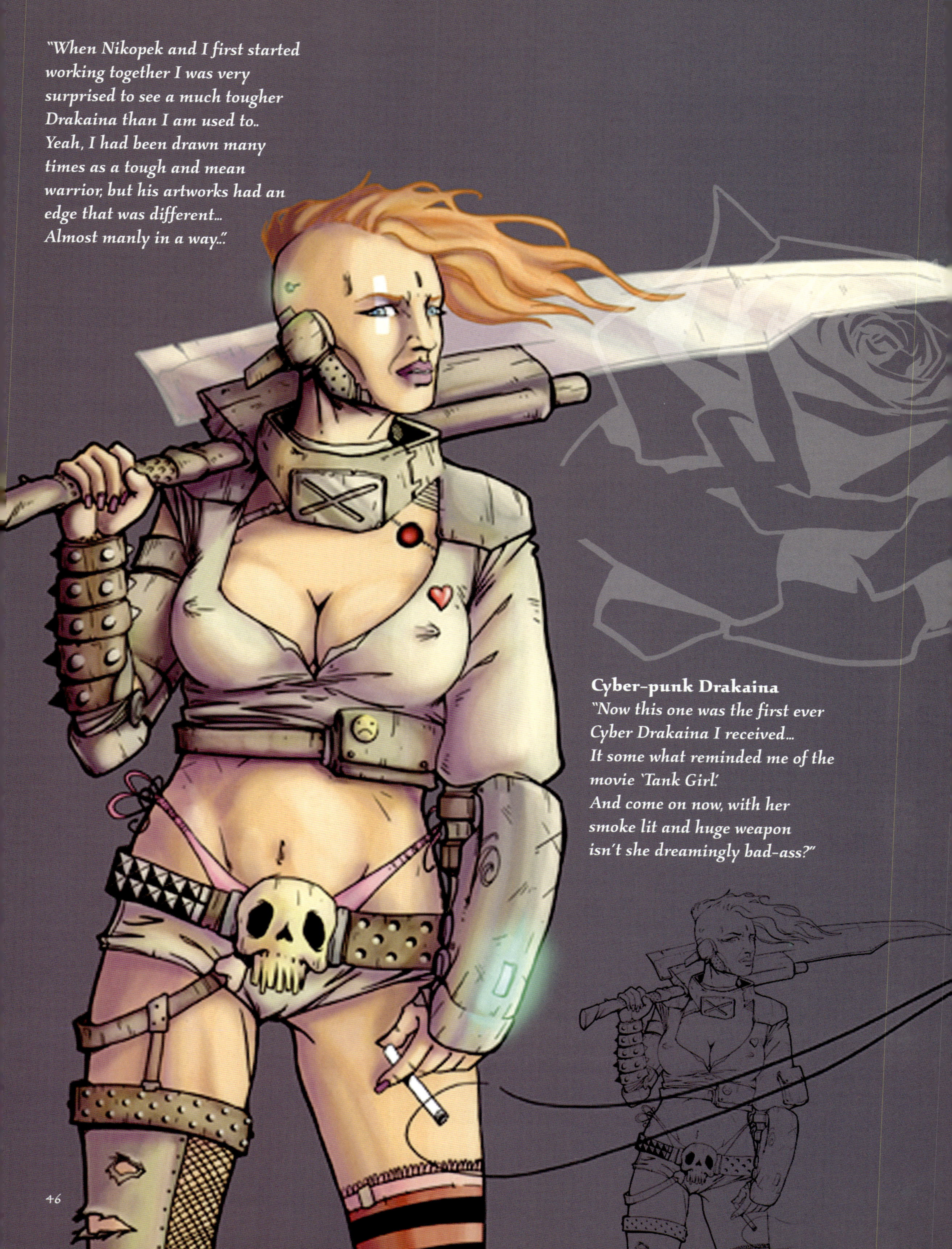

"When Nikopek and I first started
working together I was very
surprised to see a much tougher
Drakaina than I am used to..
Yeah, I had been drawn many
times as a tough and mean
warrior, but his artworks had an
edge that was different...
Almost manly in a way..."

Cyber-punk Drakaina
"Now this one was the first ever
Cyber Drakaina I received...
It some what reminded me of the
movie 'Tank Girl.'
And come on now, with her
smoke lit and huge weapon
isn't she dreamingly bad-ass?"

Drakaina by Nikopek

http://nkpek.canalblog.com/

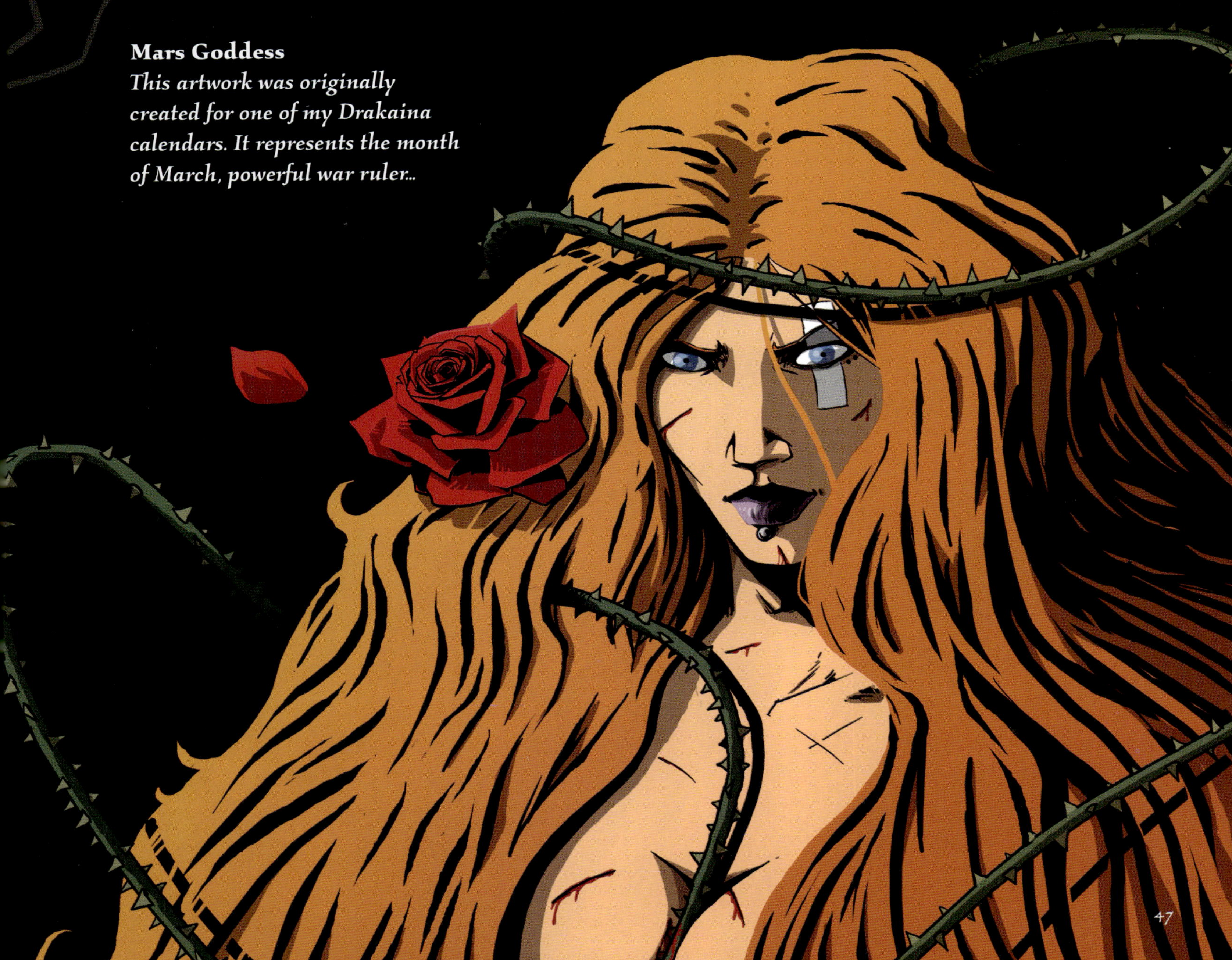

"Nikopek is a French comic book artist that I met in 2007. He usually doesn't use models as reference for his artworks but as you can see, he was quite inspired by Drakaina re-inventing her in a mix of Steam Punk and heroic fantasy"

Mars Goddess
This artwork was originally created for one of my Drakaina calendars. It represents the month of March, powerful war ruler...

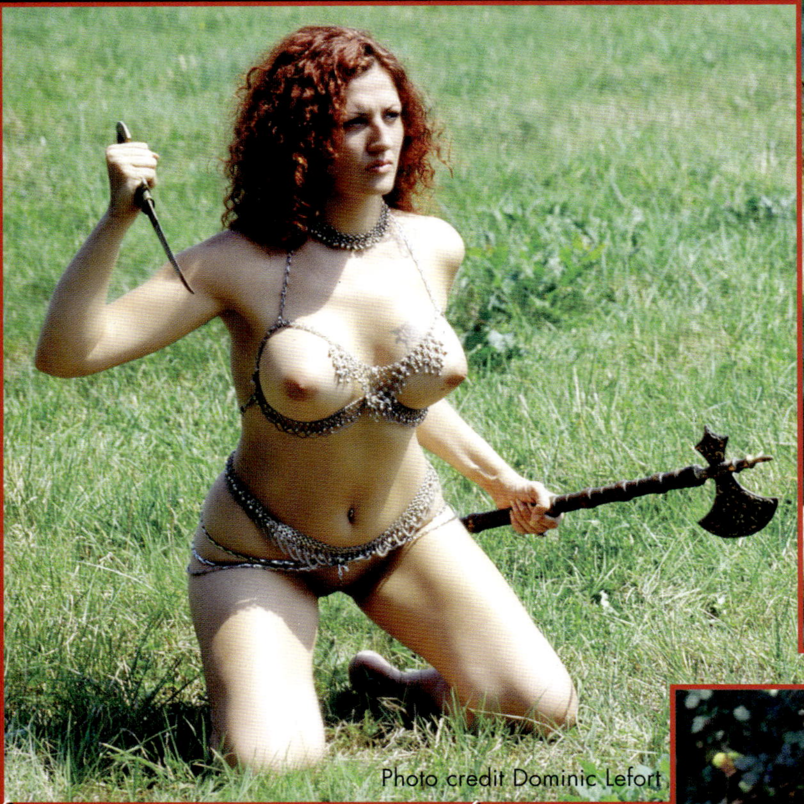

Drakaina in the Flesh

http://drakaina.com

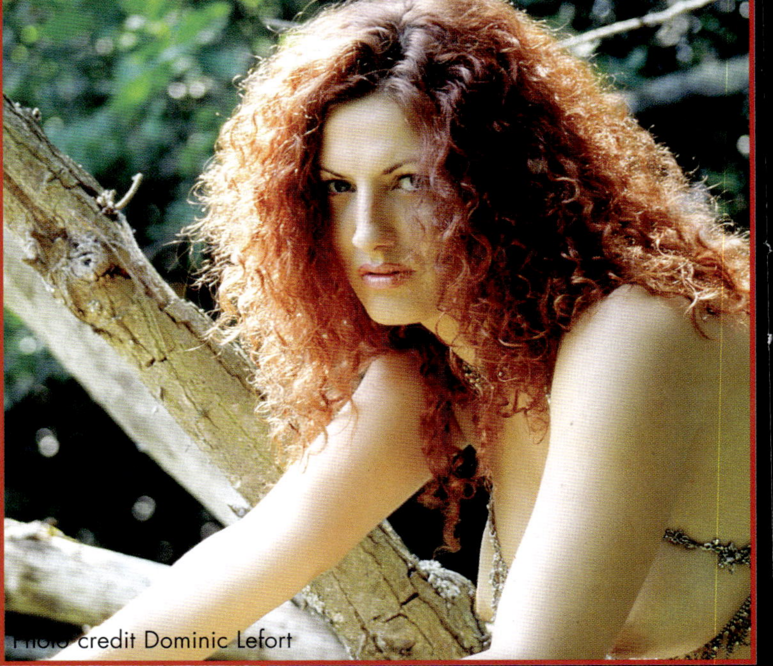

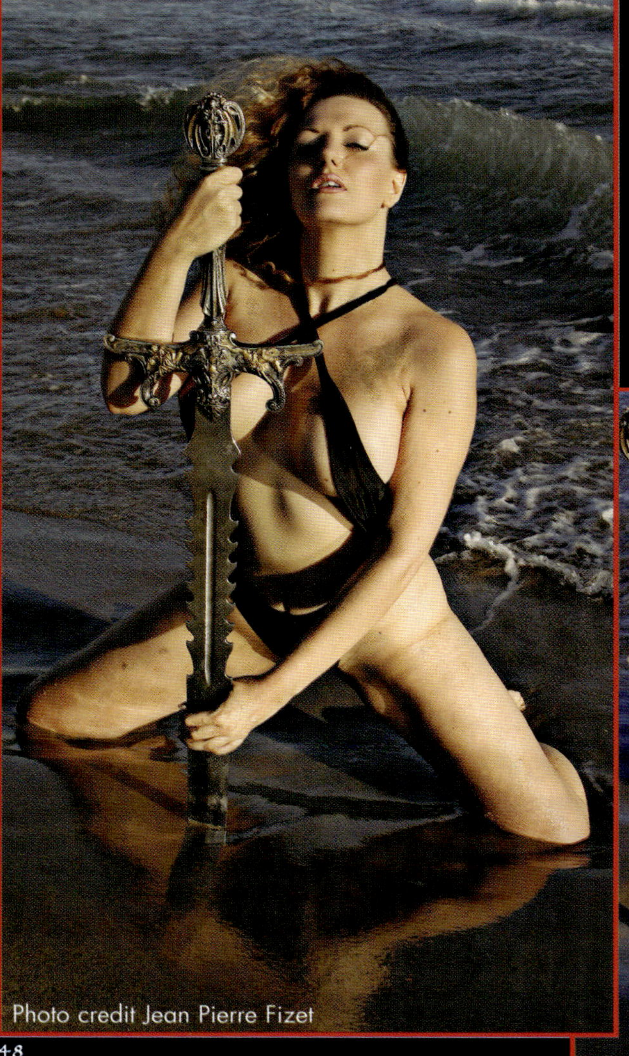
Photo credit Jean Pierre Fizet

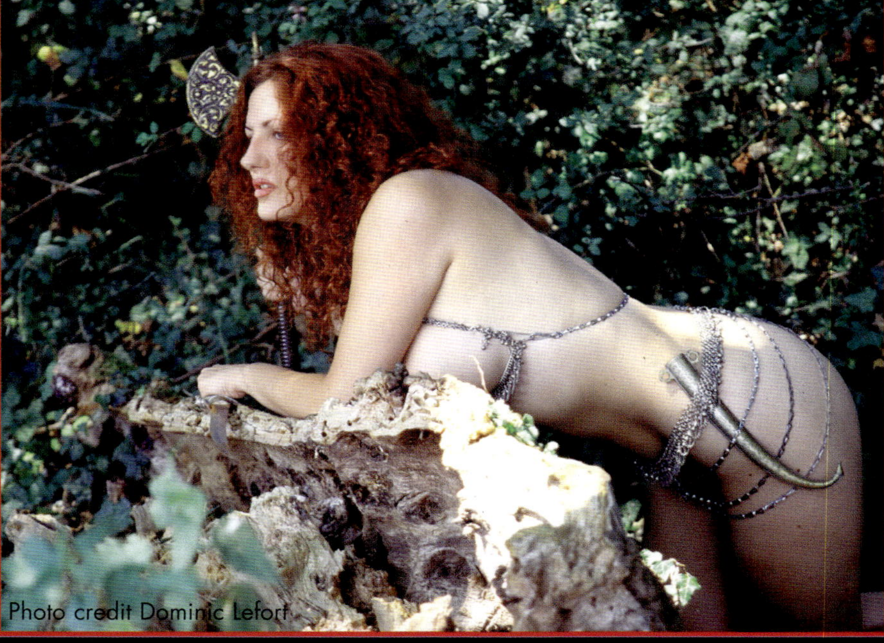
Photo credit Dominic Lefort

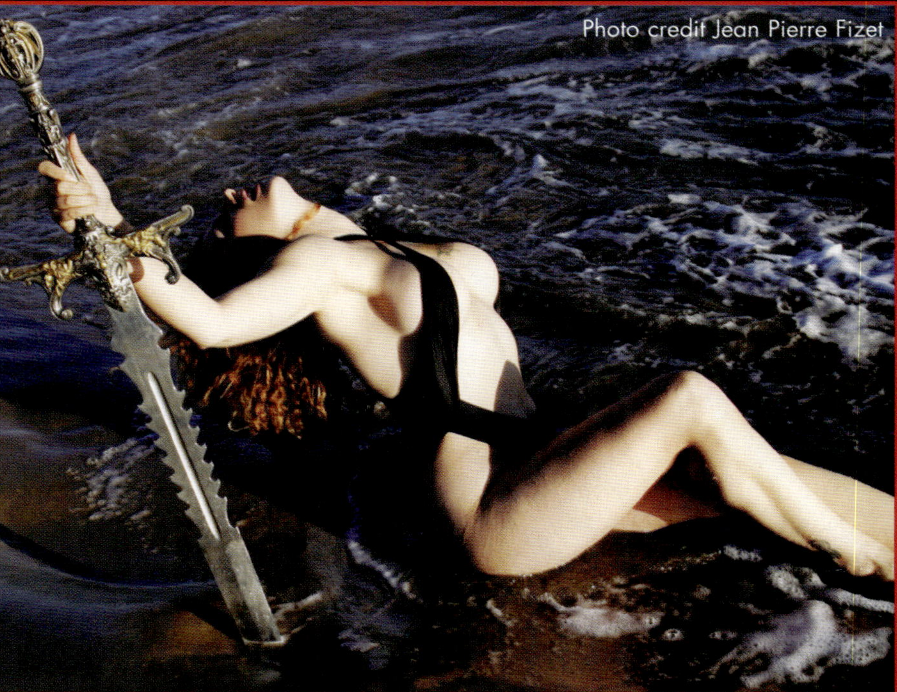
Photo credit Jean Pierre Fizet

Photo credit Dominic Lefort

Photo credit Dominic Lefort